The ten
Most Important
things
Ever Said

The ten Most Important things Ever Said

(Most Important is written over a strikethrough "ten")

Ever Said

Dan D. Schinzel

authorHOUSE®

AuthorHouse™
1663 Liberty Drive
Bloomington, IN 47403
www.authorhouse.com
Phone: 1-800-839-8640

Published by AuthorHouse   06/29/2012

ISBN: 978-1-4772-2799-2 (sc)
ISBN: 978-1-4772-2798-5 (hc)
ISBN: 978-1-4772-2797-8 (e)

Library of Congress Control Number: 2012911250

The ten most important things ever said

❖ It is your care for others that is the true measure of your greatness.
   Jesus of Nazareth

❖ A man's true wealth hereafter is the good he does in this world to his fellow man.
   Muhammad

❖ Before you embark on a journey of revenge, dig two graves.
   Confucius

❖ Let he who is without sin cast the first stone.
   Jesus of Nazareth

❖ Sacred cows make the best hamburger.
   Samuel Clemens

❖ Gentleness, self-sacrifice and generosity are the exclusive possession of no one race or religion.
   Mohandas Gandhi

❖ Treat the earth well: it was not given to you by your parents, it was loaned to you by your children.

Native American Proverb

❖ In the End, we will remember not the words of our enemies, but the silence of our friends.

Martin Luther King, Jr.

❖ You never really understand a person . . . until you climb into his skin and walk around in it.

Atticus Finch, To Kill a Mockingbird

❖ Everything can be taken from a man but one thing: the last of the human freedoms—to choose one's attitude in any given set of circumstances, to choose one's own way.

Viktor Frankl

Contents

Prologue

Nothing makes me more uncomfortable than listening to a poor speaker struggle to hold it together in front of a restless, inattentive audience. I have on too many occasions sat in just that sort of crowd, cringing as an ill-prepared presenter rambles on, repeating himself or herself over and over in between seemingly interminable pauses. In those situations, I tend to stare at my feet, unwilling to watch the unfolding train wreck. I wince as I listen to the incoherent speech, hoping the torture will soon end for everyone involved. It is only when I hear the sound of courteous applause that I can look up.

But such excruciating experiences are offset by those occasions when I hear a speaker express an idea or story or emotion with eloquence and concision. While style and delivery are important, I would argue that an entertaining, effective speech is mostly the product of good writing. A talented writer can make even a bland or timid speaker sound stirring.

Unfortunately, writing is a maddening endeavor. Most of us are unable to get out of our own way when we put pen to paper. The words we write do not seem to match the ideas we have and we end up with an unwieldy, disjointed mess. After wadding up the offending piece of paper and depositing it in a nearly overflowing wastebasket, we then stare at another blank page, hoping for some divine inspiration. (Note to reader: I have been accused of being a Luddite, as I still use a pen and paper on first drafts of my writing. For those of you whose feet are firmly planted in this century, the scene just described might be altered by referencing a delete button instead of a wastebasket.)

My inability to translate my thoughts into words leads me to produce writing that often lacks focus and is much too wordy. While I clearly understand that the most essential characteristic of an effective argument, essay or speech is brevity, I am incapable of controlling my verbal gluttony. And so out of this frustration with my own clumsy writing and speech comes a deep appreciation for those rare souls who, in a mere sentence or two, can clearly convey an idea and elicit an emotional response from a reader or an audience. These are the people we quote. The economy of their words provides us a nicely packaged expression that is convenient, versatile and easily stored, perhaps on a slip of paper or perhaps merely tucked away in our memory banks.

I love a good quote. You might call it an obsession. But my obsession with quotes is not restricted to the words themselves. I am just as fascinated with the people behind the quotes and the circumstances that inspired those people to craft their timeless words.

My captivation with the words of others is really a byproduct of my love for reading. Because I was exposed to countless great teachers and surrounded by a family of readers, I developed an insatiable appetite for the written word. Any written word. Fiction, literature, history, newspapers, backs of cereal boxes: all of these can hold my interest.

I also learned to be an active reader. I underline, take notes in the margins, dog-ear pages, all in an effort to retain ideas or phrases or even names that are of particular interest. Those who lend me books usually end up regretting it! From all this note-taking I have managed to form a fairly extensive collection of quotes and sayings that represent some of the best ideas I have come across in my reading. The ten that I have chosen for this book are taken from that collection.

Because ideas are not expressed in a vacuum, learning something about the person to whom a quote is attributed is essential if we are to fully appreciate its intended meaning. The quotes chosen for this book come from a wide variety of sources that span different cultures and times. One technique that helps me capture the context of a quote is to place myself in a scene of my creation with the author. I accomplish this historical "fantasy" simply by closing my eyes and transporting myself to the relevant place and time. I then either imagine myself as an active player in a scene, engaged in both dialogue and action with the person to whom a quote is attributed, or I assume the role of an unseen observer, a fly on the wall if you will, using all my senses to soak in the scene I have created for the person I am trying to get to know.

For this book, I ended up with ten separate scenes for the ten quotes chosen, each taking the form of a conversation involving a character created in the likeness of the attributed author. Each conversation is the creation of my imagination, a fantasy meant to expose the soul of the character while illuminating the meaning of the quote itself. Some settings for those conversations are based on either actual or apocryphal stories involving the author, while others are completely fictitious. I encourage readers to create their own conversations as well. In other words, close your eyes and fantasize as you work your way through the book.

Each quote is also accompanied by two or three relevant stories from the past: some familiar, others obscure. They are intended to further illustrate the intent of the quote. After all, history is really just a series of short stories, each complete with its own fascinating characters and unique plots and sub-plots. I first realized this in a

United States History course in high school. Great teachers leave lasting impressions and this particular teacher made the often mundane stuff of history come alive through the stories he told. The important names, dates, and places were all there but they were illuminated by stories about the bigger-than-life characters that define our heritage. This teacher did not rely on any state-of-the-art technology or faddish pedagogy. He was, simply put, a great storyteller.

And so by telling the stories I have chosen for this book, I hope to bring alive the selected quotes. The three-part approach I employ in each chapter of the book—quote, conversation and story—will hopefully provide the reader an opportunity to better understand the context and meaning of some of the wisest words ever written or spoken.

I realize that most readers will take some issue with my choices and my interpretations. A list of the most important things ever said is destined to be controversial. And any attempt to place oneself in a fictional setting with the revered figures who authored these words is bound to stir up debate. But, in the end, this book is intended to be a starting point for a conversation about how the words of the past can serve as beacons for our future. While the ten different sayings cover an assortment of subjects and are attributed to a variety of sources, they all share one common trait: the words and their meaning are timeless.

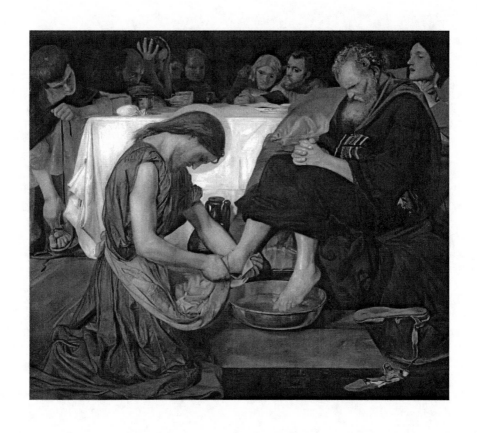

It is your care for others that is the true measure of your greatness.

Jesus of Nazareth

Act I

Sitting on a hillside near a remote village in first-century Palestine, an itinerant Jewish preacher is surrounded by his followers. He takes a child and places her on his lap. Several of the more prominent men begin to argue about who among them is the greatest.

Dialogue

♦ Teacher, we cannot decide who will have the highest place of honor in the next world. Surely one of us must rank above the rest. How should we decide who is the greatest among us?

+ Behold this beautiful child who sits here on my lap. Whoever takes care of such a child is caring for me and the One who sent me. It is your care and concern for others that is the true measure of your greatness.

♦ A child? What does tending to a child have to do with measuring our importance? Surely anyone can watch over a child.

+ *This innocent child is the work of the Father. And He has given this gift to you. No one is more vulnerable in this world than such a child. She is dependent on you for nurturing, protection, and guidance. Your unconditional love is the only hope for such a child. Just as you receive unconditional love from me, you must offer it to those who most need it from you. Your place in this world and the next is not dependent on such fleeting qualities as power, money, or even wisdom. No, your greatness lies in the care and compassion you give to those who have nothing to give you in return.*

♦ *We all agree that this child deserves the love and compassion you describe. But we also need to be practical. This world is imperfect and we need the leaders among us to assume power, grow wealth, and make decisions. Are you suggesting we can ignore the realities of the world around us and focus only on the needs of those who cannot or will not assume responsibility for themselves?*

+ *What good is a society that does not care for its most vulnerable members? Such a society glorifies those who gather wealth and power; I glorify those who give them away.*

♦ *Teacher, are you saying we must drop everything and abandon our lives and responsibilities in order to achieve the greatness you describe?*

+ *A life committed to kindness and generosity does not necessitate dropping everything. Look around you. No matter your circumstances, no matter your responsibilities, no matter your lot in life, you are confronted with countess opportunities to show care and concern for others. Extraordinary acts can emerge from the most ordinary of circumstances.*

♦ *What you say seems so simple. Yet people suffer for so many reasons: isolation, poverty, hunger, disease, abuse, oppression, to name a few. These problems are too complex for any of us to solve.*

+ *Why do you insist that a complex problem requires a complex solution? Focus on what you can control and do not worry about that which you cannot. Suffering has been a part of the world from its inception. There will always be poverty and hunger, abuse and oppression. Focus on the one who suffers rather than on the cause of that suffering. No one person can eradicate hunger, yet each of you has the power to offer a starving child a portion of what you have to eat. No one person can end oppression and violence, yet each of you can stand up for a persecuted stranger. No one person can remove loneliness and isolation from this world, yet each of you can take the time to put your arm around an outsider and make her feel welcome and loved. No one person can stop the spread of disease, yet each of you can offer care and comfort to those who are in pain. The love of my Father allows for many paths to salvation. But this I assure you: No one who has ever looked among the poor, sick, the hungry, or the forgotten, has ever failed to find me. And once you have found me, I never let you go.*

There Is Room at the Inn

Ordinary men and women, when confronted with circumstances they could never have imagined, often respond in extraordinary ways. History reveals that human beings are capable of carrying out unthinkable atrocities and inflicting indescribable pain and suffering upon one another. But history also tells us that in the presence of such evil a righteous few will emerge, armed with compassion and love, to defend the innocent victims of circumstance. This is the story of one of those righteous few.

In 1994, a 100-day genocide engulfed the African nation of Rwanda. The violence that unfolded was a product of a long history of civil unrest in the country. Ethnic distinctions between the nation's rival Hutu and Tutsi tribes provided the fuel for that unrest. In fact, prior to German and Belgian colonization, Hutus were slaves to the ruling Tutsi class. During the colonial period in the early twentieth century, differences in appearance (Tutsis tend to be tall and thin while Hutus tend to be shorter and stockier) and culture led the Belgian colonists, who took control of Rwanda after Germany was defeated in World War I, to favor the more "European" Tutsis and place them in positions of influence and power.

Conflict between the tribes mounted toward the end of the colonial period. When independence came in 1962, the Hutus took power and the country became a one-party state. The once-favored Tutsis were now an oppressed minority. While turmoil and strife were constants in Rwandan post-colonial history, the powder keg of ethnic division did not really explode until 1994, when a plane crash killed Rwandan President Habayarimana, a Hutu. The Tutsi rebels were immediately blamed.

In the wake of the death of President Habayarimana, Hutu militia began to round up and slaughter Tutsis in retaliation. Like millions of Rwandans, Paul Rusesabagina, a hotel manager of mixed Hutu-Tutsi lineage who had spent his career wining and dining generals, ambassadors, and dignitaries at both the Diplomate Hotel and the plush Hotel des Milles Collines, found himself caught in the middle of an ethnic cleansing. He and his family were suddenly surrounded by evil and forced into unthinkable situations and decisions.

The chaos eventually reached their doorstep and Hutu rebels herded Paul and his family onto a bus filled with Tutsi men, women, and children. At one point during the bus trip, he was handed a gun and told to kill the "cockroaches," a term used by the rebels to describe Tutsis. Calling on the communication and persuasion skills he had honed in his professional life, Paul managed to convince the

Hutu rebels to spare the lives of the Tutsis on board and take the bus to the Hotel des Milles, where they could be confined.

Using funds from the hotel safe, Paul was able to bribe the Hutu rebels, temporarily ensuring the safety of those Tutsis taking refuge in the Hotel des Milles. Over 1200 Tutsis eventually made it there. Once a luxurious, opulent hotel that catered to the rich and powerful, the Hotel des Milles was now a safe house for innocent Tutsis who had become the prey in a bloodthirsty genocide. Through cunning, compassion, and a little luck, Paul was able to offer hope to a desperate people.

Eventually the militia cut off electricity, food, and water at the hotel. Paul then used the swimming pool as a source of clean water and rationed the hotel food supply to ensure the Tutsis could remain there as long as possible. Outside the Hotel des Milles, the situation deteriorated badly. The United Nations presence dwindled and eventually evaporated. When rebels slaughtered ten peacekeepers sent by Belgium, the foreign forces backed out completely, essentially abandoning the Rwandan people. Paul and his hotel guests were now truly on their own. Because he was able to maintain one open phone line, Paul made daily calls to anyone outside Rwanda that he could contact, ensuring that the story of the genocide would be told even though the world had temporarily turned its back on the situation.

Eventually, Paul managed to secure transportation out of the area for the Tutsis at the hotel on a convoy by threatening to expose the rebel general in charge as a war criminal. As a result, the 1200 Tutsis who had been given shelter in the hotel by Paul escaped to refugee camps behind Tutsi lines. Men, women, and children who had been facing certain death at the hands of the Hutu rebels were safe thanks to the compassion of one extraordinary man.

The hell that was the Rwandan genocide lasted for 100 days. Over 800,000 Rwandans were slaughtered in the insanity. Yet, amidst the unspeakable horror of this ethnic cleansing, a quiet, unassuming, and compassionate hotel manager of mixed heritage ensured that none of the 1200 Tutsis who made it to his inn were among the casualties.

Could You Patent the Sun?

For those of us who did not experience the polio scares of the 1940s and 1950s, it is difficult to appreciate fully the extent of the fear and hysteria that swept the nation. The fact that so many children fell victim to the debilitating and deadly effects of polio added to the panic during the outbreak. A child who woke up one day with a stiff neck or a headache might by the next day be strapped in an iron lung, or paralyzed, or even dead. This was the nightmare endured by a generation of parents, a nightmare that turned into reality for too many families.

Polio outbreaks occurred in the United States throughout the first part of the twentieth century. A 1916 outbreak in New York City involving nearly 9000 cases caused considerable panic. Children were barred from public gatherings and the government stationed inspectors at rail stations to ensure that those who traveled had a certificate of health to prove they were polio-free.

But it would not be until the late 1940s and early 1950s that the epidemic reached its peak. By 1952, 57,000 new cases were reported. It was during this era that hysteria gripped the nation. Parents kept children away from public places and large crowds. They were not allowed to go to the public swimming pools and beaches. Misinformation about the transmission of the disease spread quickly, leading to all kinds of myths about polio. For instance, it was thought that entering cold water too quickly on a hot day or eating the wrong foods could trigger the onset of the disease.

In reality, transmission of the disease requires contact with either infected fecal material or saliva, and the virus can enter the body only through the mouth. For those living in substandard, unsanitary living conditions, the fecal-oral mode of transmission was most likely. For those in sanitary living conditions, oral-oral transmission, usually through exposure to saliva, was the primary path of infection. During the outbreak, nine out of ten people who carried the polio virus were asymptomatic and, thus, did not contract the disease. But in the remaining ten percent who did contract polio, the virus spread by way of the bloodstream and caused severe damage to motor neurons in the brain, spinal cord, and peripheral nervous system. Often, within a week to ten days of the initial symptoms of headache, muscle pain, and difficulty swallowing, the disease would progress to a point of paralysis. Images of quarantine wards filled with polio victims in iron lungs to keep them breathing, or children walking only with the aid of leg braces and crutches, highlighted the severity of this neuromuscular disease and heightened the anxiety of a public that did not fully understand the disease or how it was transmitted. Fear of the disease continued to rise in the 1950s and it soon consumed the thoughts of parents, who prayed their child would not be next victim.

Amid this panic, the medical world fervently searched for a polio vaccine. Among those engaged in the race for a vaccine was a relatively obscure virologist named Jonas Salk. After working on influenza vaccines early in his career, Salk, a doctor trained at New York University, moved to the University of Pittsburgh, where he took over the virus research lab. In 1948 Salk and his lab received a grant from the National Foundation for Infantile Paralysis, better known as the March of Dimes, to study the polio virus and develop a vaccine. Franklin Roosevelt, the nation's most famous polio victim, had founded the organization in 1938.

Salk would approach the development of a vaccine from a different angle than other labs. He believed immunity could be induced by exposure to a killed virus. Other researchers were pursuing a vaccine using an attenuated virus, one that was weakened but still alive. Salk created a process that involved killing the polio virus using formaldehyde, keeping the viral structure intact. This rendered the virus harmless but still triggered an immune response.

By 1954, as the polio epidemic raged on, Salk was ready to test his vaccine. The first human trials of the so-called Pittsburgh vaccine involved polio patients. Then, after the success of these early trials, healthy volunteers, including Salk, took the vaccination. The positive results provided great hope that perhaps polio could be conquered. The final step was a massive trial involving one million children.

On April 12, 1955, researchers released the results of this ambitious study and the Salk vaccine, as it became known, was determined to be safe and effective. Immediately, the March of

Dimes put a nationwide vaccination campaign in place. The scourge of polio was soon to be eradicated in the United States and a generation of parents could now breathe a sigh of relief thanks to the efforts of Salk and his lab.

The once-obscure scientist from the University of Pittsburgh instantly became a hero to a nation. But his greatness as a humanitarian was to surface as a result of what he said and did after his vaccine was validated. When the March of Dimes looked into pursuing a patent on the new vaccine, Salk objected, resisting the temptation to cash in on this miracle drug. In a famous interview, journalist Edward R. Murrow asked Salk who owned the vaccine. His response displayed humility and generosity: "Well, the people, I would say. There is no patent. Could you patent the sun?"

Can you imagine a pharmaceutical company today providing that response?

Eventually the Salk vaccine was supplanted by an oral vaccine created by Albert Sabin and Salk moved on to other pursuits. He would establish the Salk Institute and promote research in molecular biology. The Institute today operates over sixty labs with a variety of scientific pursuits. Salk was active in research and humanitarian causes right up to his death in 1995 at the age of eighty.

A man's true wealth hereafter is the good he does in this world to his fellow man.

Muhammad

Act II

In seventh-century Mecca, a prophet stands among an eclectic crowd that includes migrants, servants, and restless youth.

Dialogue

☪ *To surrender completely and submit your whole being to Allah is the surest route to Paradise. Those things that hinder this commitment must be set aside. For that which seems important to you now will be meaningless at the end of your life. Possessions, power, fame, social standing—all of these are fleeting.*

♦ *If these things are fleeting, how are we to measure our lives? What actions must we take to find a path to Allah?*

☪ *A man's true wealth hereafter is the good he does in this world to his fellow man. You must set yourself free from the chains of a worldly, material mindset and submit your whole being to Allah by seeking out those who are in need. To feed the destitute, to nurse the sick, to aid a stranger who has come upon hard times—these are the acts which are a measure of your true wealth. A life of charity will remain with you long after your possessions have been stripped away, long after you have lost your social standing, long after you have lost your authority.*

♦ *This is a noble ideal. It is certainly admirable to live a life of charity, but we live in difficult times. All our energy and resources must be directed toward our own survival and the survival of our families. How can we be expected to worry about the plight of those we do not even know?*

☪ *Allah has given everything to you. Prayer is your duty to Allah; benevolence is your duty to one another. You can reveal your submission to Allah by showing respect and love for your fellow man. Of course, this love must start with your family. During such complex times your own difficulties are often shared by others in your community. You will find that the love you direct toward others will return to you tenfold. For charity has no meaning unless it is a reflection of your love for Allah. All that you have and all that you are flow from that love. Just as Allah has provided shelter, food, and direction for you in your times of need, you must return the favor and shelter and feed the orphan, pity the beggar, guide those who are lost. Pray with all your soul to Allah and give with all your heart to those he created.*

Father Damien and the Lepers of Kalaupapa

For most of us, what we know of leprosy comes from the Bible. References to leprosy and lepers abound in both Old and New Testament passages. And the prevailing wisdom in Biblical times was that those who suffered from the physical and psychological effects of the disease were cursed by God. This stigma, which persisted well into the last century, was the result of fear and ignorance and was certainly fueled by the disfiguring consequences of the disease.

Leprosy, or Hansen's Disease, is a bacterial disease that is now treatable with antibiotics and preventable with proper hygiene and sanitation. However, it still pops up in impoverished areas of the world. Crowded living conditions, unclean drinking water, and poor sewage systems provide the ideal environment for the spread of the disease.

Because it attacks the nerves and skin, Hansen's disease can leave terrible scars and deformations on the face, hands, and feet. Over the course of history, efforts to contain the spread of this disfiguring disease led to the inhumane treatment of victims of leprosy. Isolated cultures were particularly fearful of an epidemic and they often took extreme steps to ensure containment, no matter the cost to the victims of the disease. It became common practice to expel those with the disease and imprison them in remote colonies.

This is the story of one of those colonies and one man who found his calling among the "unclean" outcasts that were left there to die. The backdrop for the story is one of the most beautiful places on earth: the Hawaiian Islands. Settled by Polynesians 1500 years ago, this chain of islands once existed as a loose association of small kingdoms, each of which had its own caste system. In the early nineteenth century, the islands consolidated into a single royal kingdom.

Starting in 1778 with Captain John Smith and his British entourage, Europeans began to arrive, bringing Christianity and, unfortunately, a host of communicable diseases, including leprosy, to the isolated land. As a result, the Polynesian population dropped from 300,000 in 1778 to 70,000 by the 1850s.

Because of the isolated nature of the islands, once leprosy arrived, it was a constant threat to the native population. As a result, King Kamehameha V instituted the "Act to Prevent the Spread of Leprosy" in 1866, which called for the seclusion of anyone suspected of being infected with leprosy. This law stayed on the books until

1969 and led to the exile of over 8000 victims or suspected victims of Hansen's Disease. The religious fervor and outright hostility that early on fueled this exile can be seen in the following 1877 edict from the Hawaiian Evangelical Society: "Teach every leper who wishes to remain with his own people and refuses to leave that he is sinning against human life and God's law."

The communities of Kalaupapa and Kalawao, part of an isolated peninsula on the island of Molokai, were formed into a leper colony to house these outcasts. The peninsula was the perfect site for such a colony, as it is separated from the rest of Molokai by huge sea cliffs, making it accessible only by boat or by a treacherous mule ride down a steep trail. This little piece of paradise would eventually become a prison for thousands of men, women, and children who were stripped of everything and sent there by a society that declared them unclean and unwanted.

It was just as the leprosy panic was starting to take hold that Joseph de Veuster arrived in Hawaii from his native country of Belgium. He was ordained a priest in the Congregation of the Sacred Heart in Honolulu in 1864 and became known as Father Damien. It was on the Big Island that Father Damien began his priestly vocation, traveling great distances to minister to his congregations.

Father Damien, aware of the plight of the lepers of Hawaii, volunteered to minister to the residents of the colony on Molokai. In 1873, he boarded a boat along with fifty or so lepers, and headed to the isolated colony that would become his home. Moved by compassion and indifferent to his own well-being, Father Damien had now committed his life to the service of these unwanted people.

When he arrived at Molokai, the colony was made up of over 700 leprosy victims, all of them exiled there to die. Most of the colonists could expect to survive for only a few years after they arrived. They spent that time in extreme physical and emotional pain, stripped of all dignity and subjected to deplorable living conditions. Father Damien was not the first volunteer to minister to the needs of the patients on Molokai. Many religious and health workers selflessly dedicated their lives to the care of these victims. But Father Damien became more than a caregiver. He transformed this island prison from a place lepers came to die to a place they came to live. Though ministering to the spiritual and emotional needs of the residents was his primary mission, Fr. Damien was also practical and pragmatic. He and his patients created a clean water system, bringing sanitary conditions to the island. He also built an orphanage to care for and educate the many children on the island. Under Father Damien's direction, medical care expanded and focused on improving the quality of life and combating the secondary infections such as pneumonia that ravaged the leprosy victims.

It was not enough for Father Damien to be an outside caregiver. He knew that help for these victims of leprosy ultimately had to come from one who is immersed in their circumstances. This isolated leper colony, inhabited by a people that society did not want, a people considered unclean and cursed by God, became Damien's home, the people his family.

Eventually, Father Damien contracted Hansen's Disease and he died on April 15, 1889. His words near the end, as he lay in his bed, disfigured by the disease that drew him to the island and defined his life, are those of a content and gracious man who fully embraced his fate: "I am gently going to my grave. It is the will of God, and I thank Him very much for letting me die of the same disease and in the same way as my lepers."

His was a life of compassion, humility, and gratitude carried out among a people that others wanted to forget.

American Moses

The true servants among us seem often to emerge from the most modest of circumstances. As adversity tends to strengthen character, it follows that the inclination to set aside self-interest and even self-preservation in order to care for others is more prevalent among those who come from a challenging background. The life and deeds of one humble, compassionate escaped slave from Maryland provide us with a perfect model of this thesis.

Harriet Tubman came into the world sometime around 1820 as a slave, born on a plantation in Maryland. Her birth name was Minty Ross. As a child, she first worked as a household servant but eventually moved out to the fields. Like most slave children, she received no formal schooling and would remain illiterate her entire life. Work in the fields was certainly taxing and, on many occasions, even deadly. Once while trying to protect a fellow field worker, Tubman suffered a severe injury when the overseer threw a rock at the offender and struck her on the head. As a result of the blow, seizures, narcolepsy, and headaches would plague her for the rest of her life.

In 1844, Tubman married a free black man named John Tubman and took the name Harriet. Though her owner had allowed the marriage, Tubman remained a slave. In 1849, fearing a rumor that she and the other slaves were due to be sold to settle some of their owner's debts, Tubman ran away on foot with help from a sympathetic local white woman. Moving at night and taking a route supported by the early Underground Railroad, Tubman traveled through woods and marshes to the Pennsylvania border. Eventually she made it to Philadelphia. There she found domestic work and began a new life.

That could have been the end of the story: an escaped slave making it to the North and gaining freedom. Except that Tubman was not content. It was in Philadelphia that Tubman first heard of and became involved in the anti-slavery movement. She attended abolitionist meetings and joined the Underground Railroad. Inspired by the people she met and the stories they told, Tubman decided to return to the South. Setting aside her own safety and freedom, she headed back to Maryland to get her sister and her sister's two children. A second trip followed and she guided her brother and some other slaves to the North. On a subsequent trip, she sought out her husband but found that he had remarried.

Never once considering her own safety, Tubman would continue to make trips into the South, eventually leading over 300 escaped slaves to freedom. The trips involved perilous night journeys through treacherous areas filled with slave catchers. By 1856, her exploits made her a wanted fugitive with a bounty placed on her head. One story describes how she accidentally came upon a group of white men reading a wanted poster describing her features and habits, including the fact that she was illiterate. Tubman avoided detection by pretending to read a book. She was ingenious in her planning and execution of the journeys, and she feared no one. Always on guard, she toted a gun and those she led understood she was ready to use it. Tubman was also very resourceful. For instance, she brought along light sedatives to quiet babies when silence was an absolute necessity.

Often the trips would lead all the way to Canada. The Fugitive Slave Act of 1850, which mandated the recapture and return of escaped slaves to their rightful owners, made the plight of escaped slaves more perilous, even in the North. Canada became the best option and Tubman, who earned the nickname Moses, led many of her followers all the way to Ontario.

During the Civil War, Tubman devoted herself to the cause of the Union. She went to Beaufort, South Carolina, which the Union Army occupied, and helped the former slaves there transition to a life of freedom. In addition, she worked as a spy, helping to locate targets for Union raids. On a raid she helped lead in 1863, over 700 slaves gained freedom. She acted as a nurse when called upon, and worked as a cook for the famous all-black 54th Massachusetts Regiment prior to their ill-fated raid on Fort Wagner, which was immortalized in the movie *Glory*. In short, her contributions to the war effort were varied and heroic, and once again revealed the selfless character that defined her life.

After the war, Tubman continued to work on behalf of the newly freed slaves. In fact, she would eventually transform her home in Auburn, New York into a haven for orphaned, elderly, and indigent former slaves. This was the very home which she had secured in 1862 with help from her benefactor, William Seward, who would become Lincoln's Secretary of State. She also lobbied for better education for newly freed blacks and was a staunch supporter of universal suffrage.

When asked why she seemed never to rest and continued to work so tirelessly for such causes, she replied: "Now do you suppose He wanted me to do this for a day or a week? No. The Lord who told me to take care of my people meant me to do it just as long as I live."

Upon her death in 1913, Tubman, once a slave, always a servant, received a full military funeral.

Before you embark on a journey of revenge, dig two graves.

Confucius

Act III

At the turn of the sixth century B.C. in the countryside near the state of Lu in China, an austere, yet tranquil exiled philosopher wanders along the countryside with a group of disciples. The philosopher leads a thoughtful and challenging lesson on the nature of revenge and forgiveness.

Dialogue

木 *Before you embark on a journey of revenge, dig two graves. For the revenge you seek will ultimately destroy you. If you have been wronged by another, the harm done will only be magnified if you let hate and revenge consume you.*

♦ *But vengeance is often the only way to save face, to defend one's honor, to protect one's name.*

木 *So you wish to let pride drive your quest for revenge? Let humility, not pride, determine your actions. Revenge is fleeting, forgiveness is everlasting. Revenge is emotional and controlling, forgiveness is rational and liberating. An act of revenge can be*

31

likened to tearing a branch from a tree. Once it is done, that branch can never be put back. An act of revenge will leave you broken and no amount of remorse will make you whole again.

♦ *Is there a difference between punishment and revenge? Can punishment be justified?*

木 *Punishment is done for the sake of the future; revenge is done for the sake of the past. Punishment is known beforehand; revenge is formulated afterward. Rational punishment is a necessary tool for a just society to maintain order and encourage righteousness by its members. A society that instead relies on revenge will deteriorate into anarchy. Hate and anger eventually consume people and such uncontrolled emotions spread quickly, infecting all of society.*

♦ *Might it ever be honorable to seek retribution for acts committed against others?*

木 *Consider your motivation. If you seek revenge on behalf of another, are you doing so out of compassion for the victim? Will you help the victim heal or will you create more pain? Will you help him break free of the one who wronged him or will you leave him even more powerless? Focus on the victim rather than on the senseless act that made him a victim.*

♦ *But surely those who harm the weak and vulnerable deserve to feel the same pain and suffering that they cause.*

木 *Injustice, violence, and hatred cannot be eradicated with more injustice, violence, and hatred. Rather, they must be countered with justice, peace, and love. If you observe the weak and vulnerable suffering at the hand of the strong and influential, you must act. But act out of love and compassion for the victim, not out of anger and hate for the oppressor. Seek to heal, not harm. Enough pain and suffering exist without your contribution. Besides, the greatest punishment you can bestow on those who abuse power is to stand with the oppressed. That can be accomplished only through humility and compassion. If you take any other path, bring a shovel and prepare to dig two graves.*

The Duel

Revenge, pride, ego. Mix them all together in the cauldron of politics and the outcome is certain to be as Confucius foretold. The story of the long feud and resulting duel between Aaron Burr and Alexander Hamilton, two of the nation's most prominent early statesmen, reminds us that a single act of revenge, though it happens in an instant, is often the result of emotions that have been brewing for years and that the repercussions from such acts spare no one.

The lives of Aaron Burr and Alexander Hamilton seemed destined to collide from the beginning. Hamilton, though born into a humble family in the West Indies, was blessed with talent, ambition, and a precocious mind. He eventually landed in New York City where in 1775 he joined the militia. Hamilton caught the eye of General George Washington and became a close aide and confidant to him throughout the long War of Independence. Though the two men had a squabble midway through the war that festered for some time, their mutual respect never really wavered. Hamilton eventually convinced Washington to grant him a field command and he proved himself quite an able commander during the decisive Battle of Yorktown in 1782. His wartime contributions would set the stage for his future role in the formation of the fledgling nation.

Burr, who was born into privilege (he was the grandson of the famous eighteenth-century preacher Jonathon Edwards, with whom he shared a fiery disposition), also chose military service. Interestingly enough, his experience with General Washington was very different than that of Hamilton. Burr joined Washington's staff but quickly fell out of favor as it became evident that Washington had little confidence in or need for Burr. Predictably, Burr began to resent Hamilton's status with Washington. This jealousy even prompted him to openly question Washington's leadership and wisdom. Burr was eventually moved out of Washington's camp and on to battlefield assignments.

By marrying Elizabeth Schuyler, the daughter of General Phillip Schuyler, Hamilton achieved the privileged lifestyle that Burr had come by through birthright. With this new status came power. In 1782, Hamilton won election to the Continental Congress. His subsequent experiences as an elected official under the Articles of Confederation reinforced his belief that the loose association of states that followed independence should be replaced by a strong central government.

Hamilton carried that belief with him to Philadelphia as a delegate to the Constitutional Convention in 1787. Though the Constitution created by that body fell short of his expectations (for instance, Hamilton argued for an elective monarchy with a lifetime presidential term, and he proposed that governors be appointed by the president rather than elected by the people), he campaigned with great passion for its ratification in New York. Along with James Madison and John Jay, Hamilton wrote *The Federalist Papers,* a series of essays extolling the virtues of this new, centralized government.

Once the Constitution was ratified, Hamilton became a major player in the new government. His relationship with Washington led to an appointment as the first Secretary of the Treasury. With that platform, Hamilton proceeded to lay the foundation for the country's monetary policy, a foundation that remains in place today. His major policy initiatives included the establishment of a national bank and the assumption of the debts of individual states. Proponents of states' rights, including Thomas Jefferson, abhorred this consolidation of fiscal power. The insider trading by Hamilton's network of acquaintances that preceded debt assumption led Jefferson and others to accuse Hamilton and the Treasury of promoting class warfare.

Meanwhile, Burr was forging his own path to power, albeit in a different manner and with a different agenda. When Burr left the military in 1779, he married a widow (she passed away in 1794) with whom he had a daughter. After becoming a successful attorney in New York (ironically, at one time he shared a practice with Hamilton), Burr was appointed Attorney General in 1789. Then in 1791, Burr ran for the United Sates Senate and defeated Hamilton's father-in-law, General Schuyler, who was the incumbent. The election provided the first bit of fuel for what would be a tragic feud. In fact, Hamilton vociferously questioned Burr's character during and after the election, a pattern of behavior that would continue over the next decade and a half.

Burr eventually returned to New York to serve in the legislature and help organize the emerging Democratic-Republican Party political machine. Because of his growing power and his success as a campaigner, those in Jefferson's camp sought to use Burr's influence to ensure that the presidential election of 1800 would result in a Democratic-Republican sweep of the offices of president and vice president. At the time, the candidate with the second-highest vote total in the election became the vice president. Such a sweep would marginalize the rival Federalists, in particular Hamilton and incumbent John Adams. The plan worked too well, as Burr and Jefferson ended up in an electoral tie and the election was thrown to the House of Representatives.

This unique election led Hamilton and Burr to once again collide and further fanned the flames of their feud. Hamilton had become so disenchanted with his supposed ideological ally John Adams that he had worked actively for his defeat during the campaign. When he realized that his opposition to Adams had inadvertently created the possibility of a Burr presidency, Hamilton openly supported Jefferson, creating an unlikely a political alliance between two men with incompatible views of government. Hamilton's hatred of Burr was so intense that it superseded his political principles. He went so far as to warn that disgrace would befall the country were it to elect Burr.

Due in part to Hamilton's meddling, after numerous votes the House of Representative elected Jefferson president. Burr would serve one term as vice president. While in office, he returned to New York to run for governor as an independent. He suffered a bitter loss and placed the blame on Hamilton, who had once again worked for Burr's defeat. In fact, Hamilton was almost maniacal in his opposition of Burr at this point, often slandering him in private. Of course, in politics, nothing can ever be said in private and Burr got wind of Hamilton's insults.

The stage was set for a tragic conclusion to this political feud. Revenge now replaced political aspiration as the driving force in

Burr's life. His immense pride fueled his desire for retribution and he challenged Hamilton to a duel. Hamilton's equally impressive ego precluded him from turning down such an invitation.

On the morning of July 11, 1804, accompanied only by their seconds, Aaron Burr, the sitting vice president of the United States, and Alexander Hamilton, the former Secretary of the Treasury and confidant of President Washington, the man most responsible for establishing the nation's financial system, met on a newly cleared field across the river from Manhattan in Weehawken, New Jersey to settle their differences with pistols. The two men loaded their weapons and took their positions. When word was given, both men fired and Hamilton fell to the ground. He would die a painful death the next day.

The first grave was dug. Work on the second grave soon followed.

Burr fled Weehawken. The vice president was indicted for murder but it never went to trial. After holing up in South Carolina in hopes that the whole mess would blow over, Burr returned to Washington to complete his term as vice president. Though he managed to avoid prosecution, his reputation and influence were destroyed. Burr's downward spiral continued after he left office. He eventually worked his way to Louisiana, where he began an association with

General James Wilkinson. Their intentions were never clear, but Burr would be accused of attempting to start a sovereign nation in Spanish territory. He was tried for treason and acquitted.

Though he once again had evaded punishment, Burr was now completely ruined. He was a pariah. He eventually left for Europe, settling in England. When he was ordered out of England, he returned to the United States and changed his name in order to avoid creditors. He was forced to live out his remaining years in shame.

Revenge, pride, ego.

Two graves dug.

Mob Justice

In the early 1900s, the culture of Chattanooga, Tennessee, like most Southern cities of the era, was controlled by a racist social, political, and economic power structure. Such an atmosphere of hate and fear was a remnant of the Civil War and Reconstruction era. Chattanooga had particularly deep scars from the several key Civil War battles and bitter Confederate defeats that took place in and around the area. In fact, General Ulysses S. Grant had once led Union forces into Chattanooga and routed the Confederate troops, taking control of the city and solidifying the Northern advantage in the West.

After the war, Chattanooga became a major railroad hub. Despite its growth, the community turned even more insular, driven by a blanket distrust of outsiders. Lingering resentment toward the black community dominated the social and economic fabric of the city. It was against this racially charged backdrop in 1906 that the tragic story of Ed Johnson took place.

Nevada Taylor, a twenty-one-year-old white grocery store clerk left work on January 23, 1906 and headed to her home on the grounds of the cemetery where her father was superintendent. Upon reaching the cemetery gate, an assailant attacked and raped her, using a leather strap to subdue her. Taylor was left unconscious. She eventually awoke and struggled home. Her father immediately summoned Sherriff Joseph Shipp to the house.

During interrogation by Shipp, Taylor described her attacker as short and muscular, with a soft voice. When pressed by Shipp as to the assailant's race, Taylor hesitated, saying she did not get a good look at him. Eventually, after some prodding, she told the sheriff that he was black.

With the trail getting cold, Shipp offered a $50 reward for pertinent information regarding the crime. The reward soon grew to $375. Three days later, Will Hixon, a white man who worked near the cemetery, reported to Shipp that he had witnessed a black man twirling a leather strap on the evening of the rape. Hixon later contacted Shipp again and said that he had just seen the man in question walking toward town. Shipp then tracked down Ed Johnson, a drifter who loosely fit the vague description provided by Taylor. He found Johnson walking down the road and arrested him. Hixson identified him as the man he had seen twirling the leather strap the evening that Taylor was raped.

As would be expected in a relatively small Southern community, news of the arrest of a black man who had attacked a white girl spread quickly, further fanning the flames of racism already burning in 1906 Chattanooga. Eventually, a mob of 1500 people arrived at the jail where Johnson was reportedly being held. Some were brandishing guns and lengths of rope. Demanding that Johnson be turned over to them, the mob used sledgehammers to attack the building. The National Guard, sent by the governor, eventually gained control of the situation, but the jail was heavily damaged. Judge Samuel McReynolds then addressed the mob and told them Johnson had already been relocated. To appease the angry men, McReynolds allowed five men to inspect the jail.

Indeed, Johnson had been moved earlier in the day to Nashville. Taylor would go there to identify her attacker. Johnson and another man were brought out and asked to speak. Taylor pointed to Johnson and identified him as the man in the cemetery. She claimed that Johnson's soft, kind voice was the incriminating feature.

Despite his pleas of innocence, a grand jury indicted Johnson just five days after the crime took place. The court appointed a defense team that included Lewis Sheppard, regarded as the best attorney in Chattanooga, to represent Johnson. Though the trial was set to begin on February 6, it was not soon enough for a restless white community demanding revenge. The defense team endured countless threats of physical violence leading up to the trial.

The prosecution built its case on the testimony of Taylor, Hixon, and Shipp. Taylor's testimony was a bit vaguer than that of the other two witnesses. She concluded with a rather tentative identification of the accused: "I believe he is the Negro who assaulted me." Incidentally, upon hearing that testimony, a juror lunged at Johnson and threatened to tear his heart out. He was restrained by the other jurors and, stunningly, retained his position on the jury.

Hixon, whose memory seemed to have gained some clarity by the time the trial began (likely due in no small part to the ample reward for his information), claimed he saw Jonson's face clearly due to the lights of a passing streetcar. When Shipp took the stand, he claimed that Johnson had tried to disguise his voice during the lineup.

The defense team brought Johnson to the stand and he denied being the attacker, saying he was working at the Last Chance Saloon on the night of the crime. Thirteen witnesses testified that Johnson was at the saloon at the time of the rape. The defense also went after Hixon, providing evidence that he had asked around about Johnson's appearance, implying that he had been seeking a credible suspect to turn over to the sheriff in hopes of collecting a reward.

On February 9, after deliberating for seven hours, the jury declared Johnson guilty of rape. Judge McReynolds ordered him to be hanged on March 13. Though Johnson maintained his plea of innocence, he heeded his lawyers' advice and waived his right of appeal. The lawyers feared a public lynching if the execution was delayed.

A prominent black attorney, Noah Parden, took up the case at the request of Johnson's father and informed the court that Johnson, indeed, wanted to appeal. Obviously, under the circumstances, such an appeal would be an uphill battle in either the state or federal court system. Though the unfair, almost farcical nature of the trial is obvious from our present point of view, the climate of the courts at the time made it virtually impossible for a black man convicted of a crime waged against a white woman to expect a higher court to intervene. After failing in the state courts, Parden filed a writ of habeas corpus in federal court, citing numerous violations of Johnson's constitutional rights. Precedent was not on the Johnson's side, since at the time the Bill of Rights was not considered relevant in a state trial, and the judge ruled against Johnson. He did, however, stay the execution for a week.

Parden was not through. He headed to Washington, D.C. by train and convinced Justice John Marshall Harlan (incidentally, Harlan was the lone dissenting vote on Plessy v Ferguson, the Supreme Court decision that validated the discriminatory practice of separate but equal) of the merits of Johnson's appeal, and the Supreme Court issued a stay of execution on March 18. Sherriff Shipp and Judge McReynolds were immediately informed of the decision.

Unfortunately, Johnson's original defense team was prophetic in its fears of a lynching and, ironically, the Supreme Court decision to grant an appeal sealed Johnson's doom. Driven by hate, revenge, and racism, the mob reassembled and, once again armed with guns and rope, headed for the jail. Sherriff Shipp, who after having been informed of the decision should have prepared to confront a likely lynch mob, failed to protect the jail. In fact, Shipp would not arrive at the scene until an hour after the mob first appeared. A lone jailer was on duty and a group of men easily entered the jail corridor and, after battering down some doors, took Johnson from his cell and tied him up. When he was brought outside, the growing crowd erupted and called for him to be lynched immediately. The men who held Johnson decided to take him to the county bridge.

A mob of seventy-five marched Johnson to the bridge. The frenzy grew; a rope was slung over a beam on the bridge and a noose was hung around Johnson's neck. In a headline, the March 20, 1906 *Chattanooga Times* reported Johnson's last words as "God Bless You All—I Am Innocent." Not satisfied with the pace of the hanging, the armed mob opened fire on Johnson. By the time they were done, the lifeless body contained over fifty bullets.

The short journey of revenge from the jail to the bridge was now complete, and the first grave was dug. But the story does not end here. Word of the lynching reached President Theodore Roosevelt and he ordered a Secret Service investigation of the incident. It revealed, among other things, that Sheriff Shipp was negligent in his duty and did not act with due diligence to prevent the lynching. Eventually he was indicted, along with several deputies and twenty-one of the men who made up the mob. The case against Shipp became especially noteworthy from a historical perspective because it was the first and only time the Supreme Court oversaw a criminal trial. With other matters on its plate, the Court moved the evidentiary portion of the trial to Chattanooga, where an appointed judge oversaw the proceedings. Once the evidence was presented, the trial moved to Washington and the Court rendered its decision in United States v Shipp, finding the sheriff, a jailer, and four members of the mob guilty of criminal contempt. In an unprecedented scene, the defendants received their sentences standing before the members of the Supreme Court. Shipp was sentenced to ninety days in jail.

While justice somewhat prevailed, what happened upon Shipp's return to Chattanooga is indicative of how prejudice, hate, and revenge can promote a mob mentality that obstructs all rational thought and action. After having been being found guilty by the Supreme Court of accommodating the brutal lynching of Ed Johnson, Sheriff Shipp arrived at the Chattanooga train station and was greeted by thousands of well-wishers and admirers, who serenaded him with a rousing rendition of "Dixie."

Let he who is without sin
cast the first stone.

Jesus of Nazareth

Act IV

A group of prominent religious elders surround a frightened young woman in the street. A popular teacher whom the elders view as a troublemaker comes upon the scene. The elders see an opportunity to discredit him.

Dialogue

◆ *Teacher, this woman has been caught in the act of adultery. She has sinned against God and disgraced her family. The Law of Moses says we must stone her to death. What do you say?*

+ *What motivates you to seek such retribution against this woman? What is it that makes you so passionate in your quest for justice? You reference the Law of Moses, but is that really what drives you? Perhaps other forces are at work in your hearts and minds. Maybe arrogance, power, or false piety move you. Or maybe even fear is at work—fear that your sins might be exposed and you might find yourself in the very position in which you have placed this woman. For what better way to conceal your own shortcomings than to publicly condemn the sins of another?*

♦ *Teacher, are you suggesting we do nothing to punish this woman? She must face consequences for her despicable act.*

+ *I ask you to replace your scorn with empathy. I came to care for and serve you so that you could in turn care for and serve your brothers and sisters. Do not let the letter of the law take precedent over the love and compassion that I offer.*

♦ *Teacher, are you suggesting we simply look the other way when sinners such as this woman disobey the Law? We are all righteous men and our society depends on us to enforce a respect for the Law.*

+ *Instead of seeking respect for the Law through condemnation and punishment, seek it through love and compassion. Who among you really knows this woman? Do any of you know her name or where she comes from? Are any of you aware of her lot in life? No: as you were arrogantly passing judgment over her, she became nothing more than an instrument to you, an object to flaunt your piety. She is made in the image of my Father. She is not an object to be scorned; she is your sister and deserves your love and compassion. Like you, she is not perfect. But I do not ask perfection of any of you. Instead, I ask that you seek forgiveness for your own sins and help others to do the same. Now, if I am wrong and there is even one among you who is without sin, let him cast the first stone.*

(Slowly, the elders disperse, leaving only the woman and the teacher on the street.)

+ *What happened to all those who wished to condemn you? Why did none of them cast their stones? By publicly condemning you, those self-righteous men assumed their own sins might stay concealed. But I know what is in their hearts. I forgive you, and you must now forgive yourself. You are loved by the One who made you. Go seek to repair those things in your life that have led you away from that love, and you will find fulfillment.*

Witch Hunt

The Salem witch trials: fear, false accusations, and religious frenzy all came together in a perfect storm in seventeenth-century Puritan New England, leading to one of the most disturbing periods in all of colonial history. What drove this God-fearing society to descend into paranoia and scapegoating? What caused a civilized people to resort to a literal witch hunt in order to drive Satan out of New England?

The religious and political leaders of Puritan New England believed that Satan himself was at work in their communities, operating through chosen intermediaries who lived among them. The righteous, according to the Puritan belief system, had a responsibility to mitigate the influence of Satan by exposing those who acted on his behalf. One of the most famous leaders of this intolerant brand of Puritanism was the Reverend Cotton Mather, who viewed New England as the divinely chosen Final Battlefield. His writings and fiery sermons depicted God as vengeful and controlling and humanity as depraved and unworthy, easy prey for the many demonizing forces present in the world. Such an atmosphere of fear created a society obsessed with identifying and destroying those who carried out the work of the devil. In the process, self-preservation became paramount. Men, women, and even children falsely pointed the finger at others in order to avoid having the finger pointed at them first.

This hysteria would culminate in the Salem witch trials and the public execution of twenty men and women accused of witchcraft. The story of one of those twenty, George Burroughs, provides a particularly troubling view of how, fueled by fanaticism and fear, baseless accusations can morph into accepted truths and lead to a tragic ending.

Burroughs, after graduating from Harvard College in 1670, chose the life of a Puritan minister. He took a position with a church in Maine and began his career. When his village dispersed due to the constant attacks by local Indian tribes, Burroughs landed in Salem, Massachusetts, taking over a small congregation in 1680. Though the hysteria of the witch trials was still years away, what happened during this early part of Burroughs' career helped feed the frenzy that was to come.

The church in Salem had its share of problems before Burroughs arrived, and they only intensified under his watch. The congregation was divided in its loyalty. Some approved of Burroughs and his ministry, while others vehemently opposed him. Those who opposed him made their feelings known by withholding their giving. Soon, the church faced a myriad of financial problems. As a result, Burroughs' compensation from the church was reduced, and he was vocal about his dissatisfaction with the financial arrangement.

Burroughs' first wife died during his tenure in Salem, and his personal finances would prove to be problematic as he dealt with the loss. He eventually borrowed money from a town and church leader named John Putnam, partly to pay for his wife's burial. A dispute over repayment ensued and would not be settled until after his departure from Salem. The Putnam name would figure prominently in the forthcoming accusations against Burroughs.

In 1682, Burroughs left Salem and returned to Maine where he continued to work as a minister. He eventually settled in Wells, where he led the local church and raised his seven children with his third wife. His troubles in Salem were seemingly a thing of the past and he had no contact with anyone from his former congregation.

That is until May 4, 1692 (ten years after he left Salem) when Marshall John Partridge and his men showed up at Burroughs' home while he was eating dinner with his family and arrested him for witchcraft. The posse took Burroughs back to Salem to answer to the charges made against him. Ironically, the first accusation against Burroughs had come from Ann Putnam, the niece of the man who had the financial dispute with Burroughs. She claimed to have had a dream in which Burroughs revealed that he had bewitched and killed his first two wives and was an agent of Satan, a "conjurer" of witches. She also said that in her dream Burroughs told her he had cast a spell on the troops defending his village in Maine during an attack by the Wabanki Indians.

So how did a young girl in Salem have a vision about a minister she had never met, who lived many miles away in Maine and had not been in Salem for a decade? It seems rumor and hysteria got mixed together with a little personal vendetta. Though Ann Putnam was too young to have known Burroughs when he was in Salem, she had probably heard of him through a servant named Marcy Lewis, who had lived with the Burroughs family in Maine. Because of the aforementioned dispute over money during Burroughs' time in Salem, it is also likely she had heard her uncle, John Putnam, speak of the minister in unflattering terms at some point as well. The accusation that Burroughs cast a spell over the troops may have seemed plausible because Burroughs always escaped harm during the many Indian attacks endured by his settlement. In the Puritan mindset, the devil was at work among the Indians, and the fact that Burroughs managed always to come away from the attacks unscathed proved he was an agent of Satan.

The hysteria began to spread and the accusations against Burroughs continued to mount. The young Lewis girl testified that she had a vision of Burroughs carrying her to a mountain top and tempting her, much as Satan had done to Jesus. Another young girl claimed Burroughs had given her dolls that had magical properties. And a young man who spoke with Burroughs when he was first incarcerated accused him of casting an evil eye upon him, resulting in strange visions. Others spoke of Burroughs' renowned physical strength and speed, that he was able to carry heavy barrels of cider and able to travel vast distances in short periods of time. Burroughs did himself no favors by answering these charges of superhuman powers by claiming his feats were easily matched by an Indian acquaintance of his and, thus, not significant. As noted earlier, the Puritan settlers viewed Indians as being in cahoots with the devil.

The evidence against Burroughs was heavily dependent on dreams and visions. Such spectral evidence had been prominent in other witch trials that preceded the Burroughs trial. Shortly after Bridget Bishop was the first of the accused to be hanged at Gallows Hill on June 10, 1692, Cotton Mather wrote to the Salem court urging them not to rely on spectral evidence in theses trials, as such visions might be the work of the devil as well. But the hysteria had taken hold, and the rush to cleanse New England of Satan and his agents led to further trials and hangings.

Burroughs was convicted of witchcraft and, on August 19, authorities brought him to Gallows Hill to be hanged. Present among the crowd was Cotton Mather, who would witness his first and only execution of an accused witch. Apparently his concerns over spectral evidence did not preclude him from watching Burroughs meet his fate. As he stood at the gallows, Burroughs made one final claim of his innocence and then recited the Lord's Prayer, which, according to Puritan tradition, no agent of Satan could do. Many in the crowd then began to believe in his innocence and demand his release. But Reverend Mather reminded the crowd that the devil could wear many disguises, and the execution went forward.

Despite not having set foot in Salem for a decade and despite the absence of any real evidence beyond that of the anecdotal, spectral variety provided by easily influenced young girls, Burroughs was put to death at the end of a rope for being a conjurer of witches, another casualty of the hysteria that swept through Puritan New England.

By the time the last stone was cast, there were twenty innocent victims put to death on Gallows Hill, each one killed by rumor and innuendo.

Holy War

The 1980s had it all: MTV, the Rubik's Cube, the end of the Cold War, the awe of the first Space Shuttle flight and the devastation of the Challenger disaster, a miracle on ice (Olympic hockey) and a miracle underground (the rescue of Baby Jessica from a well in the middle of Texas). The 1980s also had religion. This decade saw the billion-dollar industry known as televangelism reach its zenith, as the airwaves filled with flamboyant preachers competing for big ratings and full collection plates.

One of the most indelible images of the decade was that of disgraced televangelist Jimmy Swaggart appearing in front of millions on his weekly television show with a white-robed church choir as a backdrop, tearfully telling the world: "I have sinned against you and I have brought disgrace and humiliation and embarrassment upon you. I beg your forgiveness." How Swaggart ended up in this rather uncomfortable position is a lesson in hypocrisy. Casting stones can, as Swaggart discovered, lead to an ugly downfall.

During the 1980s, mega churches began to pop up everywhere. Preachers such as Jerry Falwell, Pat Robertson, Jim Bakker, and Jimmy Swaggart quickly made the transition from local pastor to national celebrity by using television as a medium to grow their empires. Stations across the country began to air these flamboyant televangelists. The programs usually featured the dapper preacher standing in front of an adoring congregation on a pristine stage, dressed in a finely tailored suit. With a Bible in one hand and a microphone in the other, they spewed out fire-and-brimstone sermons reminiscent of God-fearing Puritan ministers of a bygone era. And, of course, a toll-free phone number would scroll across the bottom of the television screen in case the viewer at home was moved to provide a little financial support for the cause. The House of God may not have become a Den of Thieves, but it did accept cash, check, or major credit card.

No one could deliver a good old-fashioned fiery sermon better than Jimmy Swaggart. His combed-back hair and emotion-filled facial expressions, complete with a little sweat on the brow, created just the right visual to complement his oratorical flourish. His sermons had the perfect cadence, with dramatic pauses interrupted by almost violent outbursts. As he railed against moral decay, Swaggart would highlight the shortcomings of those responsible for poisoning the Christian way of life. His rants against homosexuality, adultery, and pornography were expressed with a level of sincerity and authority unmatched by any of his peers. He could the scare the devil (and a few dollars) right out of the adoring audience.

Swaggart's ministry made him rich beyond his wildest dreams. At the peak of his popularity, he was taking in $150 million per year, mostly from contributions. He owned a Lear jet and a spacious vacation home. His Assemblies of God Church in Baton Rouge seated 7500. Swaggart Ministries reached 195 countries and 8 million viewers each week through his television empire. Swaggart even started his own Bible College, which grew to have an enrollment of over 1400. In short, he had it all: fame, fortune, and an adoring congregation of faithful followers.

Swaggart had certainly worked hard to get to the top. He was, in a sense, a self-made success. Born and raised in Ferriday, Louisiana, in a devout Pentecostal family, he began his preaching career in the 1960s after being ordained in the Assemblies of God Church. Swaggart began to make a name for himself by doing radio. His original show was called "The Camp Meeting Hour" and it attracted a modest audience throughout the Bible Belt. Swaggart then established his church in Baton Rouge, and it grew steadily throughout the 1970s. By the close of the decade, his congregation had grown to over 1000.

But it would be television that would ultimately make Swaggart the face of evangelical Christianity. He began to broadcast a weekly hour-long program on a local station that, by the mid-1980s, had expanded to over 3000 stations. The show originally featured Swaggart at his Family Worship Center, but it soon expanded to include his many "crusades" filmed at different locations throughout the country where his fiery, emotional preaching style attracted a "rock star" quality following. Realizing the power of television, Swaggart added a daily Bible study show called *A Study in Word.*

In the heyday of televangelism, Swaggart had established himself as the top dog. But others had strong ministries as well. The evangelical market was getting crowded and Swaggart was looking for any opportunity to marginalize the competition.

In 1986, Swaggart told Assembly of God church officials that Marvin Gorman, a successful minister in New Orleans who was growing his own television empire, had committed adultery. He pressed those church officials to defrock Gorman and strip him of his ministry. They did, and Gorman lost everything. This was good for Swaggart in the short term, as a potential rival was eliminated. But Gorman, as we will see, did not go away quietly.

Soon after Gorman was exposed, Jim Bakker of the PTL Network had his famous fall from grace. Bakker's affair with church secretary Jessica Hahn became tabloid fodder, and once again Swaggart had helped to engineer the downfall by pressuring the Assembly of God church officials to remove Bakker. On Larry King's television talk show, Swaggart infamously called Bakker a "cancer on the body of Christ."

Clearly, Swaggart was now in control. The moral shortcomings of his rivals had been exposed at just the right time. Nothing could possibly stop Swaggart Ministries. The empire seemed indestructible.

Then, in March of 1987, Gorman filed a $90 million defamation lawsuit alleging that Swaggart and others had spread false rumors in order to bankrupt him. Gorman had admitted to a single extramarital affair. But, according to the lawsuit, Swaggart and his wife Frances had contacted members of Gorman's congregation and told them that their pastor had engaged in multiple affairs. The lawsuit was eventually dismissed, forcing Gorman into bankruptcy. But he was not finished with Swaggart yet. Gorman hired a private investigator to look into some anonymous tips he had received that Swaggart was frequenting a strip club outside New Orleans that was known for prostitution and drugs. Gorman's private investigator hit pay dirt when he caught Swaggart in a tryst with a prostitute at a Lake Charles, Louisiana motel. He took pictures and then called Gorman, convincing him to come out to the motel. In a scene not even Hollywood could create, the investigator let the air out of Swaggart's tires in the motel parking lot. As a result, when Gorman arrived, he found Swaggart, dressed in a sweat suit, trying to change his tire.

A decisive counter punch had been struck in this Holy War. Even the slick-talking Swaggart could not find a way out of this mess. Faced with such overwhelming evidence, he eventually confessed to those same Assembly of God Church officials whom he had convinced to remove his rivals that he had engaged in an illicit affair with a prostitute and had battled an addiction to pornography his whole life. In an effort to absolve himself of responsibility for his actions, Swaggart blamed Satan and his sex addiction for his poor decisions. Of course, Swaggart would have dismissed such a defense as ludicrous had it come from Gorman or Bakker.

And so, in February of 1988, Jimmy Swaggart took the stage in his Baton Rouge church and, in front of a television audience of 8 million, made the tearful confession that would cost him an empire. The irony of Swaggart's precipitous downfall was not lost on his audience or the general public. Swaggart became the face of hypocrisy in a decade filled with it.

Eventually, Swaggart would return to the pulpit with the same fire and determination as before his downfall. The stones began to fly once again. But, of course, he had not changed. In 1991, Swaggart was pulled over in a seedy neighborhood in southern California. Sitting in the passenger's seat was a prostitute.

Sacred cows make the best hamburger.

Samuel Clemens

Act V

On a warm summer evening in late nineteenth-century Connecticut, two men are sitting on the porch of a large Victorian home, staring at the chess board that lies between them. The older of the two men puffs on his cigar and laughs. The younger man looks up at his amused opponent.

Dialogue

♦ May I ask what's so funny?

You sure are wastin' a whole lotta time thinking about moving one of those pieces. We sit out here night after night making the same moves in the same order with the same pieces and then we can't quite figure out why every game ends in a draw. Just make the move we both know is comin' and let's get on with the game.

♦ Well, if you know what I am gonna to do before I do it, how come you can't beat me?

Like you, I am as stubborn as a mule. You know damn well that my next move ain't changin' either, no matter how long I stare at that board.

♦ *I guess trying something new just ain't in our nature.*

A more inflexible creature than man has never walked the earth. We never change. Despite making the same mistakes over and over, we human beings inevitably stick to the way things have always been done. We just ain't comfortable tryin' new things.

♦ *Well, any words of wisdom before I make my move?*

Consider this: Sacred cows make the best hamburger. Now hurry up; I ain't getting any younger.

You can have any color you want, as long as it is black

Henry Ford is considered among the most influential industrialists of the twentieth century. His rise to wealth and prominence is one of the great American success stories. The Ford Motor Company emerged from a crowded field of automobile manufactures at the turn of the last century to monopolize the industry. It was Ford's willingness to break with conventional wisdom and embrace new ideas and new ways of doing things that was the impetus for that early success.

Yet, ironically enough, the growth of the Ford Motor Company eventually came screeching to a halt because Henry Ford seemingly forgot what got his company to the top. Somewhere along the way, stubbornness replaced creativity and the once-dominant carmaker lost control of the market because he refused to abandon his sacred cow, the Model T.

Ford was born and raised on a farm near Detroit, Michigan in 1863. Despite his father's wish that he take over the family farm, Ford eventually left and headed to Detroit, where he became an engineer with Edison Illuminating Company. It was while he was at Edison that Ford began to tinker with engines and automobile design. Working in his kitchen and in a shed in the backyard, he eventually built a prototype automobile with an internal combustion engine and, in 1896, drove it out onto the streets of Detroit.

Of course, Ford did not invent the automobile. Nor did he invent any of its components. In fact, by 1900 over thirty manufacturers were producing automobiles. And though in that same year only 8000 autos were out on the streets of the United States, the number of companies seeking to enter the market exploded. Almost 2000 firms would produce one or more automobiles in the next decade. Such intense competition among so many proprietors was due in part to the ongoing debate over whether steam, electricity, or gasoline could best power the engines in automobiles. Nearly $400 million in start-up capital would be invested in new automobile firms.

With the help of a few investors, Ford started the Detroit Automobile Company in 1899. This first attempt at entering the market failed, and the company dissolved. Ford, using his engineering prowess, continued to design and build prototypes. Then, in 1903, with about a dozen investors and only $28,000 in start-up capital, the Ford Motor Company was born. The company originally produced 1700 cars in three models. They were expensive, but his shareholders insisted on sticking to the conventional business model that said a better bottom line was dependent on a high per-unit profit margin.

This was the same strategy employed by every other automaker at the time, and Ford recognized that his company would not be able to emerge from the pack unless it took a different approach. After taking control of the company from his other investors, Ford abandoned the prevailing high price-high profit paradigm and produced an affordable, universal car for the multitudes. To meet his goal of placing the power of mobility in the hands of the average American, Ford cut profit margins and refined his plant production line to ensure maximum efficiency. The result was the Model T, the car of the people, which in 1908 rolled off the assembly line with a price tag of $825. Ford Motor Company sold 10,000 units that first year.

In order to achieve his objective of producing an inexpensive car while growing company profits, Ford needed to devise a more efficient assembly process. Early on, the company's plant produced its Model T in the traditional manner: a group of mechanics would build a car from scratch at one station. Ford realized the best way to meet increasing demand and lower production costs was to develop an assembly line that enabled workers to specialize in one task. Instead of having a car produced at a single station, Ford designed his plant to accommodate a moving assembly line. Each of the four floors of the plant specialized in one part of the assembly process, creating a division of labor that greatly increased production efficiency.

Such specialization lessened the need for skilled laborers. Critics went so far as to suggest it turned workers into robots. Other industries that employed assembly lines used this move to unskilled labor as an excuse to cut wages. Ford once again ignored conventional wisdom and instead increased his minimum wage to an unprecedented $5 per hour. He also instituted a forty-hour work week. Keeping labor costs low was a sacred cow in industry at the time, and Ford's competitors criticized these changes as careless and irresponsible business practices.

But the changes proved to be economically savvy. The employee turnover rate, long a problem in the auto industry, decreased markedly at the Ford Motor Company, and the savings in worker training costs more than made up for the increased wages. Furthermore, by raising the standard of living of his workers, Ford created a new pool of potential buyers for his affordable Model T.

By 1921, over sixty percent of the cars on the road were Model Ts. Ford had essentially cornered the market. His plant was able to produce a car every twenty-four seconds, and in 1924 the ten millionth Model T rolled off the assembly line at the absurdly low price of $290.

Ford's willingness to think outside the box had led him to this point. And that is what makes the rest of the Ford story truly baffling. Inexplicably, ingenuity gave way to complacency, causing the Ford Motor Company to lose its steely grip on the automobile market.

By the mid-1920s, the market had changed. It was now several decades after the introduction of the automobile to mainstream America, and consumers demanded innovation. Other automakers such as General Motors and Chrysler offered variety in style and a host of amenities in their new automobiles. They also introduced the concept of payment plans to help average Americans finance these more luxurious cars. Ford refused to adapt to the changing market. His Model T, available only in black, with its outdated shifting pattern and original four-cylinder engine, became much less appealing as other automakers flooded the market with cars of better style and substance. The all-black Model T, once a ubiquitous sign of American progress and ingenuity, quickly turned into a relic.

Ultimately, the marketplace forced the Ford Motor Company to end production of the Model T in 1927. The man who once famously wrote that the customer could have his car painted any color he wanted, as long as it was black, either had to give in and meet the demands of the consumer, or see his company fail. Thanks to some forward thinking by Ford's son Edsel, the company was able to retool its factory and quickly launch a new line of automobiles that could compete with the other big automakers. But the domination of the market that the Ford Motor Company once enjoyed was no longer possible. It was now a competition among the Big Three—Ford, General Motors, and Chrysler—and the innovation that followed in the auto industry would be driven by the consumer rather than the producer, something that Ford probably never imagined when he rolled that first Model T onto the streets of Detroit.

Henry Ford, the great innovator, built a car for the people. It was his greatest achievement. Refusing to part with that sacred cow became his greatest failure.

Outsmarting Big Blue

In this age of handheld electronic devices, it is easy to forget that a generation ago, computers that had less memory and speed than a smart phone took up entire rooms and required a staff of programmers to run. In the 1960s and 1970s, computers were considered to be exclusively a tool for big business. IBM (International Business Machines) dominated the computer industry, building mainframe computers for corporate clients. These mainframe computers were high-performance, centralized units that were bulky and expensive.

The name mainframe comes from the large metal frames that housed the computers in their designated room. Every department in a business would share the same mainframe and its programmers, creating an inefficient, cumbersome system for delivering technology.

Big Blue, as IBM was known, had a firm grip on the mainframe market. No one could compete with the computer giant. That dominance even led to an anti-trust lawsuit in 1969. The suit alleged that IBM unfairly eliminated competition in the mainframe market by bundling services, limiting choice, and releasing misinformation about its computers. The suit eventually was thrown out, but it, along with some other legal issues, ended up sapping IBM of a lot of money and resources.

The reputation of IBM as a stodgy, inflexible behemoth was certainly well deserved. The company had grown at such a rapid pace that by the 1970s, IBM seemed invincible. To the executives in charge, the mainframe computer, the cash cow of the company, was the future. There was no need to diversify, no reason to pursue innovation or explore new markets. IBM was seemingly in control.

At about the same time Big Blue was reaching its peak, the nascent personal computer industry was gaining steam. Small, innovative technology companies began to pop up, among them Apple and

Tandy. These companies saw huge potential in the home computer market. They envisioned a personal computer that would be easy to use, convenient to set up and maintain, and versatile enough to be used for a variety of tasks, including office work, games, and information processing. This vision of the future of technology was in stark contrast to that of IBM.

The personal computer revolution really began in earnest in 1977 with the introduction of the Apple II. A vast improvement on an earlier model, the Apple II was a ready-to-run microcomputer that was user-friendly and contained such amenities as a keyboard and color graphics. The Tandy TRS-80 showed up on the scene in the late 1970s as well. Its large memory, floppy disk drive, and game software made it quite popular.

While all this home computer innovation was happening among these smaller computer companies, IBM sat on the sidelines, clinging to the view that the personal computer was nothing more than a passing fad. The bigwigs at IBM were protective of their sacred cow—the mainframe computer. After all, they argued, a computer is a business machine that is too complex to market to the average American.

Mistake number one.

As the decade of the 1980s opened, the personal computer market was exploding. Technology once reserved for banks, big business, and universities was now packaged into a convenient, user-friendly machine, and the consumer demand provided huge profits to companies like Apple and Tandy. Personal computers became such the rage that in 1982 *TIME* magazine named the computer as its Man of the Year.

Eventually Big Blue had no choice but to acknowledge the profit potential of the personal computer and enter the market. But they knew that their entry into the market would be costly. IBM's focus on the mainframe industry had left them way behind in developing both the hardware and the software for a personal computer. They knew they had to move quickly, even if it meant compromising sound business practices.

Mistake number two.

In 1980, IBM engineers began working on Project Chess with the objective of developing a new computer that was code named Acorn. Being so far behind the curve in research and development, IBM made a production decision that was counter to company policy. Because of its vast resources, IBM never outsourced any part of research, development, or production. If Big Blue needed something that another company held, it simply purchased the whole company. But the clock was ticking and IBM needed a personal computer to put on the market quickly. So when it came time to find an operating system to run the Acorn hardware, the powers that be at IBM decided to outsource.

IBM initially tried to reach a software deal with Gary Kildall of Digital Research, Inc., who had developed an operating system called CP/M. Though there is much debate about the actual details, industry legend suggests that Kildall blew off the meeting with the executives from IBM and went flying in his airplane. Whatever happened, this much is definitely true: because IBM left without signing on Digital Research, not many people know Gary Kildall, and everyone knows Bill Gates.

In the 1970s, Gates and his partner Paul Allen had started a small software company called Microsoft, in Seattle. After the fiasco with Kildall, IBM executives met with Gates and Allen, who proposed a deal whereby Microsoft would provide an operating system for the IBM personal computer. Gates and Allen stipulated that Microsoft would retain ownership of the software and be able to market it to other companies. Such an agreement was anathema to basic IBM business principles. It made no sense for the most powerful company in the country to hand over control of a key component of production to some fledgling software company. They held all the cards and could have simply bought out Microsoft right then and there. But the decision-makers at IBM, clinging to the past, believed that there was no value in software and the real worth of any computer lay in the hardware.

The real irony of this is that Gates and Allen did not even have an operating system in hand when they negotiated the landmark deal with IBM. So in this poker game with the suits from IBM, they were playing without any chips!

No problem. After signing the exclusive deal to provide an operating system for the new IBM personal computer, Gates and Allen simply went out and found one. They bought a system from another Seattle-based company for $50,000 and renamed it MS-DOS. There was nothing special about this particular operating system, as its designer had simply used Kildall's system as a model.

In 1981, the IBM PC with MS-DOS hit the shelves and was an instant success. It became the leader in the personal computer industry, primarily because the IBM name gave the product credibility with consumers. By 1985, IBM had 40% of the PC market. And every time an IBM PC sold, Microsoft made money. Because it outsourced its operating system, IBM had not only lost a fortune, but also any stake it might have had in the growing software industry. Gates and Allen knew the real profits in the personal computer industry lay in software and that other smaller computer companies were positioned to produce faster and more powerful computers more quickly than IBM. And, of course, because Microsoft retained ownership of MS-DOS, they were free to sell it to any computer company that came along.

Companies like Dell, Hewlett-Packard, and Compaq chipped away at IBM's share of the personal computer market, producing better and better computers, all with Microsoft's operating system, at cheaper and cheaper prices. By 1989, IBM had only a 17% share of the PC market and it continued to shrink. The once-indestructible giant soon found itself in financial trouble before reorganizing in the 1990s and refocusing on software and services.

Microsoft has made both Bill Gates and Paul Allen billionaires, and the company now has the supremacy in the technology world that was once held by IBM. A couple of computer geeks with no leverage, no money, and no product in hand went toe to toe with the most powerful company in the country and ended up taking control of the computer industry right out from under it.

All because Big Blue was blinded by an allegiance to its sacred cow, the mainframe computer.

Gentleness, self-sacrifice and generosity are the exclusive possession of no one race or religion.

Mohandas Gandhi

Act VI

A balding, bespectacled, older man wearing a traditional Indian pancha emerges from a train and walks out on the elevated platform amidst a bustling crowd. At his side is a younger man dressed in similar fashion. As the older man walks briskly along, his sandal slips off his left foot and falls through the platform to the lower level of the train station. He stops and ponders what has happened. He then removes the sandal from his right foot and drops it through the platform as well. The young man turns to his older companion with a look of confusion.

Dialogue

♦ *Why did you toss away your other sandal? With some luck, we may have been able to retrieve the first sandal that fell through the platform.*

Perhaps. But it is more likely that someone below would have found the sandal first. And is it not better that the one who happens upon the sandal have the other one as well? What good is one sandal?

♦ *But that was your only pair of sandals. You must now walk barefoot while a stranger makes off with your sandals. For all you know, the man who finds the sandals might be a thief or a political enemy.*

Or he might be a beggar or an outcast or simply someone who is in greater need of that pair of sandals than I am. Whoever finds them is now better off. It is important that our generosity does not have boundaries. We cannot place conditions on our compassion.

♦ *But is it not our duty to help first those who share our heritage, those who share in our suffering and oppression, those who share our religion?*

Look beyond such barriers. To reserve your empathy for only those who think, feel, and believe as you do is selfish and empty. To reach out to those who are of a different religion or espouse a competing political philosophy or have a different complexion or speak another language—that is real compassion.

♦ *How can we be expected to show compassion for those who belong to a culture or religion that does not share our beliefs?*

No culture or religion has all the answers, but I believe they all seek the same truth. Kindness and compassion are central to all faiths. So do not ask our Christian or Muslim brothers and sisters to think or act like Hindus. Instead, ask our Christain brothers and sisters to be better Christians. Ask our Muslim brothers and sisters to be better Muslims. I honor the faith of others, just as I honor my own.

♦ *It truly does not matter to you who it is that who picks up your sandals. How can I move beyond my petty prejudices and insecurities and achieve such a selfless existence?*

Set aside religious dogma and cultural biases and nurture your faith through service to others, as that is where true meaning is found. For gentleness, self-sacrifice, and generosity are the exclusive possession of no one race or religion.

Corrie Ten Boom

Following the 1940 German invasion of Holland, the occupying Nazi regime began to systematically round up Dutch Jews, rob them of their possessions, pack them like animals onto trains, and transport them to concentration camps. For Dutch Christians, the best hope for survival during the occupation was to remain silent and look the other way as the Nazis carried out this purge. After all, the German authorities viewed the Dutch Christians as an Aryan people who merely lacked the necessary indoctrination. In other words, in the eyes of the Nazis, to be Dutch was a pardonable offense. To be Jewish was not.

Keep quiet and stay alive, or offer help to the Jews and risk everything—even the lives of your family. Not an easy decision. Yet many made the choice to act, and the Dutch Underground became a lifeline for fleeing Jews and other dissidents. No one risked more than Corrie Ten Boom and her family.

Born in Haarlem, just west of Amsterdam, in 1892, Corrie Ten Boom was the youngest child of a watchmaker. She and her three sisters and one brother lived with their mother and father in a residence that sat above the ground-floor shop that served as the family business. Members of the Dutch Reformed Church, they were devout in their Christian faith. Corrie would remain single her whole life, but found her calling in her father's profession. She became the first female watchmaker in Holland. She also devoted her time and energy to community service, acting as a leader in clubs for girls and working with families of the mentally disabled.

Everything changed when the Nazis overran the country in 1940. The way of life that Corrie had known her first forty years was no more. Because the Nazis wished to "win over" the Dutch people, the initial occupation may have been less intrusive for Dutch Christians than it was for those in other countries that had fallen to the German army. But restrictions on food, movement, and news eventually affected everyone.

For the estimated 140,000 Jews in Holland at the time of the invasion, things quickly deteriorated. By 1941, the deportation effort was in full swing. Eventually, nearly 110,000 Dutch Jews would be sent to camps. The remainder went into hiding. It is estimated that only around 5000 of those deported would survive and return to Holland.

Without hesitation, Corrie and her family became active in the Dutch Underground, even though they knew that any contact with Jews could jeopardize the freedom and safety of a Christian family like theirs. Once the deportation policy took effect, harboring a

Jew made one an enemy of the state. But despite such danger, the Ten Boom family began taking in Jews. Some of those who sought shelter stayed only a few hours, while others stayed for months. Corrie, through some connections she developed when she was doing volunteer work, was able to procure food ration cards in order to feed those hiding in the house.

Corrie also began to convince other Dutch Christians to act on behalf of the Jews, and she soon developed a network of safe houses. Of course, not all Dutch Christians were convinced that helping the Jews was prudent. In her book *The Hiding Place*, Corrie tells of a visiting pastor whom she asked to shelter the baby of a Jewish family that was hiding in the house. He refused, saying that a Christian should not risk his life for the life of a Jewish child. Her father then picked up the baby, looked at the pastor and said: "You say we could lose our lives for this child. I would consider that the greatest honor to come to our family." To Corrie and her family, compassion and sacrifice were not reserved for any one particular race or religion.

Those Jews who found shelter at the Ten Boom house were treated as guests. Because of their strong belief that Jews were God's Chosen People, Corrie and her family had tremendous respect for the Jewish faith and its customs. The Sabbath and the major holidays became part of the household routine. Corrie and her family even provided kosher food when possible.

The family built a hidden room behind Corrie's bedroom on the upper level of the house by surreptitiously hauling in bricks and other materials. The secret room was constructed at the highest point inside the house because it would be the last area to be searched, providing more time for those in hiding to get inside. The finished room was ventilated, and accessible only by a hidden entrance behind Corrie's closet. They also installed a warning system that would signal those hiding in the house to go to the secret room if the Nazi authorities showed up.

In 1944, the room and warning system were put to use during a Nazi raid on the house. Tipped off by an informant, the German authorities searched the house. The four Jews in the house at the time managed to get to the hiding place. They remained silent and in the dark for forty-seven hours, evading the search party.

The Nazi authorities arrested the entire Ten Boom family after the raid. Eventually, the family was split up and members would meet varying fates. Corrie's father, already frail, died in custody ten days after his arrest. Her sister Noll and brother Willem gained their release. The Nazi authorities sent Corrie and her oldest sister Betsy to Ravensbruck concentration camp in Germany. The abuse and suffering eventually were too much for Betsy, and she died at the camp. But because of a clerical error, prison officials eventually released Corrie. Fate was certainly on her side, as a mass extermination of the women at Ravensbruck occurred soon after her departure.

After the war, Corrie continued to live a life of service and compassion. She established a rehabilitation center for victims of the war. She also began to speak and write of her experiences, eventually authoring several books, including *The Hiding Place* and *Tramp for the Lord*. It was in the latter work that Corrie wrote of a 1947 encounter with a former guard from Ravensbruck. He had been particularly brutal and sadistic and had sought her out to ask her forgiveness. Corrie describes clasping the man's hand and "feeling God."

Jewish tradition suggests that only the blessed have the honor of dying on the anniversary of their birth. In 1983, Corrie Ten Boom died on her 91st birthday.

Transcendent Peace

On November 19, 1977, a plane landed at Ben Gurion Airport outside of Tel Aviv, Israel. This particular plane was unlike the hundreds of other planes that came in and out of this busy international airport every day. When the door to the plane opened, Egyptian President Anwar Sadat emerged. As he stepped on to the tarmac, he became the first Arab leader ever to visit Israel. Waiting to greet him was Israeli Prime Minister Menachem Begin. An astonishing scene: two men, sworn enemies from two different worlds, representing cultures and religions that had clashed for a thousand years, leaders of once warring countries, clasping hands. A Muslim and a Jew together in Israel, seeking peace and understanding. What led to this historic meeting and what would follow is a testimony to the resolve of these two remarkable leaders, a resolve that sought to transcend the barriers of race and religion in order to establish peace.

Since its inception in 1948, the state of Israel has precariously carved out an existence under the constant threat of violence and war. The surrounding Arab states, including Egypt, refused to recognize Israel's right to exist. The conflict in the Middle East was and is essentially a religious one. The Arab states claim that all of Palestine rightfully belongs to the Muslim people, as it is written in the Quran. This, of course, runs counter to not only the Jewish tradition of the Promised Land found in Hebrew scripture, but also the United Nations partitioning plan, which created the state of Israel. So surrounded as it is by hostile neighbors, Israel has been forced into a series of confrontations with its Arab neighbors in order to preserve its very existence. Out of necessity, Israel has developed a strong military with the help of Western allies, especially the United States.

War is almost a way of life for the country. For instance, Israel fought four separate wars with Egypt, resulting in a series of occupations and border changes. The non-stop military conflicts are really battles within the larger cultural and religious war that began with Israel's establishment in 1948. Two battles are of particular pertinence to our story of Sadat and Begin. In June of 1967, the Six Day War began as Egypt, Jordan, Iraq, and Syria all began to make aggressive moves with their respective armies, threatening Israel's borders. Gamal Nasser, the Egyptian leader, established a naval blockade and initiated troop movements in the highly volatile Suez area south of Israel. The armies of Jordan, Syria, and Iraq began to make advances from the east.

Faced with the prospect of an invasion, Israel, under the leadership of Defense Minister Moshe Dayan, initiated pre-emptive attacks.

The Israeli air force quickly took control of the sky and destroyed the enemy air forces. On the ground, the Israeli army pushed the Egyptians back across the Suez Canal, destroying their tanks and artillery. In the north, the Israelis had similar success, driving back the Syrian forces and capturing the Golan Heights. They also routed the Jordanian army and seized the West Bank. Israel had not only prevented an invasion, but had taken over the Sinai Peninsula from Egypt, the Golan Heights from Syria, and the West Bank from Jordan. While the military victory was decisive, the addition of the new territories would become problematic because of the presence of hundreds of thousands of Arabs in these now-occupied lands.

In 1973, the Arab alliance would attempt to regain the lands lost in the Six Day War. What became known as the Yom Kippur War began with a surprise attack by Egyptian forces in the Sinai and Syrian forces in the Golan Heights on the holiest day of the Jewish calendar. The strength of the Arab attack can be attributed both to the huge numbers of troops deployed by Syria and Egypt and to the financial support of other Arab nations. The acquisition of aircraft and other Russian weapons greatly strengthened both armies, making the attack quite devastating.

Initially, Egypt and Syria enjoyed great success. Egypt crossed the Suez Canal and entered into the Sinai while Syria made gains in the Golan Heights. However, within a few days, Israel mounted successful counter attacks in both the Sinai and the Golan Heights, pushing the Arab armies back. They even managed to cross the Suez Canal and start moving toward Cairo. The Israeli military had overcome the initial shock of the attack and taken control of the occupied territories, essentially routing the Syrian and Egyptian armies. The United Nations eventually stepped in and a cease-fire was declared after nineteen days. Israel would maintain control of the Sinai Peninsula, which was a strategic victory in that it provided a buffer zone in the south, helping to ensure that future military action would not occur on Israeli soil. The Golan Heights also remained in Israel's control. The United Nations stationed troops there to ensure peace along the border between Israel and Syria.

The campaign was a complete failure for the Arab world, especially Egypt and its leader, Anwar Sadat. The Israelis had fought a war on two fronts against two feared Arab nations and scored an overwhelming victory, despite being caught off guard by the initial attack. It was initially unclear how Sadat would react. The famous shuttle diplomacy of the United States as carried out by Henry Kissinger helped move Sadat in the direction of a peaceful settlement of differences with the Jewish state. But Sadat faced pressure both within Egypt and from other Arab states to continue to seek a military solution that would ensure the destruction of Israel. Muslim fundamentalists throughout the Middle East were committed to reclaiming all of Palestine. To them, negotiation and compromise with the Jewish state of Israel was a betrayal of the Arab cause.

Yet Sadat, drawing upon the kind of courage and resolve found in too few political leaders, replaced Egypt's long-standing military approach to Israel with a diplomatic one. In 1975, Egypt and Israel signed an agreement to formally pursue a peaceful resolution to their differences. Despite the refusal of Syria and Jordan to join in the process, Egypt and Israel, with the United States acting as a mediator, engaged in dialogue and negotiation that would eventually lead to Sadat making the unexpected announcement that he would travel to Israel in November of 1977.

So the unlikely scene at Ben Gurion Airport came to be. And just as remarkable a scene would occur in Egypt the following month as Begin reciprocated with a visit to the city of Ismailia. Leaders of two countries, once sworn enemies, were breaking barriers once thought impenetrable. After taking office in 1977, President Jimmy Carter ratcheted up the role of the United States in the peace process, ultimately bringing Begin and Sadat together at Camp David, the presidential retreat in Maryland, for thirteen days of talks. Eventually the two leaders would sign the Camp David Accords, which would lead to the 1979 Israel-Egypt Peace Treaty.

There were many extraordinary images from these unprecedented meetings. But the most enduring and most instructive image came at the White House when the agreement was signed by Sadat and Begin and witnessed by Carter: Standing together were three men of differing faiths, nationalities, and cultures clasping hands and smiling, sharing a moment made possible by a shared hope for peace.

Unfortunately, the story does not end there. Sadat would lose his life because of his commitment to peace. He was gunned down in Egypt during a parade by a group of fundamentalist army officers who viewed him as an enemy of the Arab cause.

Ironically enough, while both former President Carter and Prime Minister Begin led the American and Israeli delegations to Anwar Sadat's funeral, only one Arab state, Sudan, sent a representative.

Treat the earth well: it was not given to you by your parents; it was loaned to you by your children.

Native American Proverb

Act VII

A young girl sits at the feet of her grandfather as he slowly rocks in his chair. They are on the porch of his home on the plains to the east of the Black Hills of South Dakota. As a member of the Lakota tribe, the grandfather hopes to pass on to his granddaughter the traditions and heritage of their people.

Dialogue

Our ancestors came to this land because of the trickery of Inktomi, the devious spirit. The Lakota once existed beneath the earth. In the form of a wolf, Inktomi led one of the Lakota men to the land above and showed him the green pastures, the abundant resources and clear sky. Inktomi then showed the tribesman the herds of buffalo and promised that they would provide plentiful food for the Lakota people. When the tribesman reported back what Inktomi had revealed to him, our ancestors emerged from the earth and the hills. But they had been misled by the devious spirit, for the resources were not endlessly bountiful. However, our people learned to cultivate the land and hunt the great *herds of buffalo with a respect that ensured Mother Earth would prosper and provide the Lakota people with food and shelter.*

◆ *Grandfather, how do we teach others to share our respect for nature?*

Reverence for the Creator demands that we care for his creation. The land, the sky, the air we breathe and the buffalo we hunt do not belong to any one person or any one tribe. They belong only to the Creator. We are the stewards of these gifts and must take only according to our need and always restore when we are able.

◆ *What happened to our land? The beauty of the grasslands, the herds of buffalo, the pure air and sky are all gone.*

The modern world views man as the rightful owner of the sky, the water, and the land. We accumulate and consume instead of share and conserve. Respect for the Creator no longer means respect for the creation. The buffalo that sustained our people are no longer thriving, because of our greed. The grasslands and forests have disappeared, because of our selfishness. The air is no longer pure and the water no longer clear, because of our gluttony. The belief that nature's bounty is a gift from the Creator to be respected and conserved has been replaced by the belief that creation is a mere commodity to be exploited according to our wants.

♦ *Grandfather, can we ever return to the ways of our ancestors?*

Perhaps, but we must first realize that our actions not only show a disrespect for the Creator but also endanger the well-being of our children and grandchildren who will inherit this earth from us. Our ancestors said it this way: Treat the earth well: it was not given to you by your parents; it was loaned to you by your children.

How to Make a Sea Disappear

Water is our most precious resource. Water brings life. Take it away and life falters and is eventually extinguished. Even small changes in freshwater availability can drastically affect the balance of any ecosystem. So what would happen if an entire inland sea disappeared? An ecological disaster.

Millions of years ago, what is present-day Uzbekistan and Kazakhstan was completely covered by a massive body of water. Over the course of time, the waters slowly receded, leaving the Aral Sea (which means Sea of Islands, so named because of the many small islands that dotted the water), unique not only in its size but also in its ecosystem. It was a massive inland saltwater sea fed by two freshwater rivers, the Annu Darya and the Syr Darya. Its low salinity was conducive to a wide variety of aquatic life. The sea was at one time home to sturgeon, catfish, pike, and other important species of fish. This diversity led to the growth of a prosperous fishing industry that became the economic backbone of the region. The rich ecosystem also gave rise to abundant populations of waterfowl and mammals.

It was in the mid-nineteenth century that Russians first began to explore and utilize the Aral Sea. Because the Aral Sea was inland and not connected by waterway to the ocean, ships had to be brought in over land and assembled on the sea. Once the Aral Sea was mapped, the fishing industry began to flourish, and seagoing vessels dotted the water. Fishing towns began to pop up along the shore, among them Moynuk and Nukus to the south and Aral to the north. Eventually thousands of locals would carve out an existence in and around the Aral Sea. At the height of its prosperity in the mid-twentieth century, the Aral Sea provided close to 15% of the Soviet fish production. In addition, because the ecosystem provided such a beautiful and diverse natural surrounding, a thriving tourism industry emerged in the harbor towns.

For many years in the area surrounding the Aral Sea, the local population, relying on knowledge of and respect for this unique ecosystem, managed to live off the land and sea without depleting it of its resources. The people of the Aral Sea region understood that a balance could be achieved that allowed for a vibrant human presence without destroying the natural beauty of the land or sea.

Then everything changed in 1960s. The Soviet government, in the midst of the Cold War, embarked on a program to improve agricultural production as a means of asserting economic and productivity superiority over the West. In particular, there was a push to become self-sufficient in cotton and rice. Such a plan, of course, required exploitation of the country's natural resources, and the Aral Sea region was the prime target.

In order to create suitable farmland in the region, the government needed to create an irrigation system using the freshwater flowing into the Aral Sea. Engineers dammed up the Amu Darya and the Syr Darya Rivers, cutting off the freshwater supply to the Aral Sea. Canals were built to divert the water to the land around the lake, turning a once-arid land into plush farmland, ready to be exploited by the Soviet government in order to meet its productivity goals. The plan to increase the rice and cotton output of the country was underway.

The consequences of blocking the freshwater supply to the Aral Sea and flooding the plain were immediate and devastating. In the 1960s, the sea began to undergo a rapid transformation. The water level fell precipitously and the shoreline receded at an alarming pace. The Aral Sea, which had covered 26,000 square miles prior to the dam project, lost 75% of its volume and 50 feet of its water level. Harbor towns such as Moynuk that were built on the shore ended up as far as sixty miles from the depleted sea. These once-thriving communities eventually turned into boarded-up desert towns. The Aral Sea, once one of the four largest inland bodies of water in the world, soon became so depleted of water that it dried up and split into four separate lakes of limited depth and volume. By 2010, further loss of water led to the disappearance of one of the four lakes and the reduction of another into little more than an elongated pond.

The destruction of the flora and fauna that depended on the sea occurred quickly. The fish populations were virtually wiped out due to the loss of water and to the increased salinity of what remained of the Aral Sea. With the freshwater supply cut off by the dams, the salt level of the sea became toxic to any species of fish or plant that might have survived the drop in water level. The increased use of pesticides and fertilizers in the newly irrigated farmland led to contamination of the canals, rivers, and lake, contributing to the killing off of not only the fish and aquatic plants, but also waterfowl and mammals. A once-diverse ecosystem was reduced to an environmental wasteland.

By the early 1980s, the commercial fishing industry completely shut down in the region. The livelihood of thousands of fishermen disappeared, and a vibrant local economy was reduced to nothing. The only remnants of the industry today are the numerous abandoned fishing boats that are rusting away on dusty, arid land that had at one time been covered by the Aral Sea.

The destruction of the Aral Sea has also impacted the health and well-being of the inhabitants of the region. The land exposed by the shrinkage of the lake has become dry and dusty. The pesticides and fertilizers get whipped into the air along with the dust. This has led to a marked increase in respiratory problems and cancer rates. The dry, polluted air has also been linked to a higher infant mortality rate. With the diverting of the river water to the system of canals irrigating the plains, there has also been a rapid dwindling of the drinking water supply. And the fresh water that is left has been contaminated by the pesticides and fertilizers.

There is some hope that the Aral Sea can be restored, at least to some degree. The construction of a dam between what are now the northern and southern lakes has led to increased water levels and lower salinity. Efforts to restock the lake with fish have seen some success. But there is little hope that the Aral Sea can ever recover to the point of once again being a vibrant and unique ecosystem. The short-sighted policies of a government intent on exploiting the natural resources of the region for immediate economic gain are to blame for this ecological disaster. No mitigation project can undo the damage done to the water, land, flora, and fauna of the region. A way of life defined by respect for and conservation of the natural resources that sustained it is unlikely to be restored. It, unfortunately, disappeared along with the sea.

The Death of Easter Island

Remote and mysterious, Easter Island is best known for the strange, enormous statues that the Rapa Nui people carved out of the island's dark rock. But this small volcanic island in the South Pacific, 2000 miles west of Chile, is also of interest because of the ecological and societal collapse that occurred there as a once-thriving ecosystem was reduced to desolate grassland, and a once-vibrant culture was driven to near extinction.

Easter Island, so named because it was "discovered" by Dutch explorer Jacob Roggeveen on Easter morning in 1722, offers us yet another example of how the appearance of Western explorers brought doom and destruction to a native population through disease, slavery, and theft of the land.

It is generally agreed that the first inhabitants of Easter Island were Polynesians who traveled there by canoe over thousands of miles of ocean sometime between 400 and 500 A.D. The island that these first inhabitants found contained a unique landscape. It was a conglomeration of three extinct volcanoes. The only freshwater supply came from the lakes associated with these volcanoes. A mixture of trees, shrubs, and grasses covered the island. Pollen studies of the sediment strata indicate that the most abundant tree was the palm. These palms would have produced a bounty of nuts that probably served as a staple food source for the settlers. Also abundant were species of tree ideal for producing rope and firewood. There were no mammals on the island, but several species of sea birds thrived there due to the lack of predators. The fish population, though limited due to the cool water and the rocky coastline, still provided some food.

The first settlers spread over the entire island and began to cultivate the land and grow food. The soil was not rich, but was adequate for growing certain crops, chief among them sweet potatoes, which became a staple of the islanders' diet. Archeological studies of bones indicate that the abundant porpoise population in the waters around the island served as a primary source of meat. In addition, the colonists brought chickens to the island. Chickens had long been a domesticated animal in other Polynesian settlements.

Unfortunately, the inhabitants also brought over another animal, this one uninvited. Rats appeared on the island with the first settlers and they quickly proliferated, free of predators and able to feed off the seeds and nuts of the forested island. Due to their increasing numbers and efficient gathering techniques, these rats began to strip the island of its ability to regenerate.

The steady destruction of the forest began to take its toll. The settlers cleared land for a variety of reasons: farming and gardening, firewood, construction of canoes, production of rope and nets. This rapid clearing of trees, combined with the destruction of seeds and nuts by the growing rat population, caused the forest to shrink, leaving the soil prone to erosion. But it would be the building of the mysterious statues that would prove to be the final death knell of the fragile ecosystem.

The Rapa Nui people on Easter Island developed a culture and power structure based on ancestry. They lived in clans. In order to facilitate rituals based on this ancestral hierarchy, each clan began to construct the now famous head and torso statues called Moai. Craftsmen carved these giant statues out of the black volcanic rock. Because this process required a certain type of rock, the craftsmen all worked on the statues at a single site. Once completed, the giant statues had to be transported to the over 360 platforms, or Ahu, constructed by the clans throughout the island. Such a move often involved many miles and rugged terrain. The sheer size of the statues complicated the task even further. The average weight of the Moai was fourteen tons. And since each clan sought to outdo rival clans, a competition ensued and the statues grew larger and larger. The largest extant statue on the island is close to eighty-two tons.

The exact mechanics of the transport process is debatable, but it is certain that it required copious amounts of wood to accomplish. It is most likely that tree trunks served as giant rollers. The movers would have laid these trunks on the ground and pushed the giant statues along, perhaps using long wooden poles. Once the statue arrived at the Ahu, it would then be lifted onto the platforms using levers.

The competition to carve and erect larger and larger Moai almost certainly led to the destruction of the oldest and largest trees on the island. The palms eventually disappeared and the landscape began to change over time. The pressures on the forest were now numerous (the clearing of land for farming, the need for firewood, the building of canoes and nets for fishing and, what may have been the final straw, the moving and erecting of the statues) and the ecosystem began to collapse.

As the landscape changed, the social structure of the island began to unravel. The lack of resources caused the clans to alter the ancestral power structure and abandon the rituals that defined it. The construction of the statues came to a halt. Archeologists have uncovered many incomplete statues left at the carving site, and even some completed statues seemingly abandoned en route to their destination. Survival became the focus of the clans as resources dwindled. The population of the island crashed and, with wood at a premium, the clans began to use caves as shelter. By the time of the first contact with Europeans, the prestige of building bigger and bigger statues had given way to more practical and urgent issues related to survival. In fact, when Roggeveen arrived in 1722, he found what he described as a barren island supporting a population of only 2000-3000 natives. At its peak, the island had over 7000 inhabitants. He also noted that many of the statues were toppled over. Scientists suggest that rival clans began to topple the statues during the many conflicts that occurred during the societal upheaval.

Predictably, the arrival of Europeans led to exploitation of the native population. Slave traders arrived in the middle of the nineteenth century and captured and hauled away many of the Rapa Nui people. Epidemics of smallpox and tuberculosis led to the deaths of hundreds of islanders. Missionaries established settlements on the island and began to buy up the land from the native population. Chile eventually assumed control of the island and it became home to a vast sheep-raising operation. Incidentally, the presence of the sheep further damaged the already depleted landscape. The one hundred or so Rapa Nui left on the island found themselves confined to a few designated colonies, and their living conditions deteriorated so profoundly in the early twentieth century that an uprising ensued.

Eventually, the Chilean Navy took control of the island, leading to further isolation and exploitation of the native population.

Today, Easter Island is completely open and the remaining Rapa Nui are considered Chilean citizens. Many of the statues have undergone excavation and restoration. And with the addition of an airstrip, the island is much more accessible, thus removing some of the mystery that once surrounded Easter Island and its history.

The restored statues provide a connection to the past on Easter Island. Once thought to be mysterious objects placed there by a mysterious people, these vestiges of a collapsed culture are now reminders of how fragile an ecosystem can be. The natural balance that ensures regeneration is easily upset by the activities of man. And on an isolated island, the results can be devastating.

The Deadliest $1 Ever Spent

In the late 1970s, Love Canal, a serene, middle-class community in Niagara Falls, New York, found itself at the epicenter of an environmental disaster when a ticking chemical time bomb lurking beneath the soil exploded, threatening the lives and property of those living there. The ensuing events would reshape public environmental policy and serve as a rallying point for those who fight to protect our land, water, and air from the poisons man so cavalierly produces and discards.

The Love Canal community owes its inviting name to William Love, an entrepreneur of the late nineteenth century who sought to create a self-sustaining community by digging a canal off of the Niagara River. This waterway would provide cheap energy for a development of new homes and businesses. Unfortunately for Love, such water-driven energy was quickly made obsolete by the discovery that alternating current could be efficiently transmitted over long distances. By the close of the first decade of the twentieth century, Love was bankrupt. He abandoned the project and left only the partially dug canal.

Soon, the empty canal became a chemical dumping ground. It was assumed that the clay soil that made up the walls of the canal would sufficiently seal in any disposed-of chemicals. A large company named Hooker Chemical started to use the site for disposal of the many waste chemicals coming out of its plants. Hooker dumped thousands of tons of toxic chemicals into the empty canal, including carcinogens such as DDT, dioxin, and mercury. At the time, such dumping practices seemed innocuous, especially since the area was very sparsely populated.

Eventually, Hooker Chemical filled in the canal and covered it with clay, again assuming that the chemicals would be safely sealed in by the soil. Finished with the site, Hooker sold it to the city of Niagara Falls in 1953 for one dollar. This seemingly generous contribution of land to the community by a local industry would initially be hailed as a shining example of corporate philanthropy, a model of how a business-community partnership can work for the greater good. In time, however, the deal would be exposed as the most expensive one dollar that any community may have ever spent.

The board of education soon built a school on top of the landfill and over one hundred homes sprouted up around it. A working-class community now sat directly on top of the buried waste disposal site. For the next twenty-five years the quiet neighborhood would grow. By the mid-1970s, the school had over 400 students and the neighborhood contained more than 800 homes. The residents went about the business of raising children and living their lives, while beneath them a perfect chemical storm brewed, slowly seeping to the surface, awaiting an opportunity to completely erupt.

Signs of trouble had been surfacing for years. Reports of strange odors, skin irritations, and the appearance of chemicals bubbling to the surface popped up soon after the school was built. But it was in the late 1970s that more serious problems began to emerge. Likely triggered by a couple of unusually rainy years, chemicals began to leach out of the soil. Large metal drums filled with chemical waste surfaced as the ground washed away. Backyards and swimming pools became awash in chemicals. The smell intensified and reports of children suffering minor burns and eye irritations began to circulate.

Thanks to the crusading actions of a local mother named Lois Gibbs, residents began to document illnesses. Miscarriages, birth defects, and abnormal white cell counts were occurring at high rates. Gibbs and other residents began to realize that something was seriously wrong. The entire neighborhood was being poisoned by what was now leaching through the soil. Nothing was safe—not their homes, not the drinking water, not the air they breathed.

Soon the press got involved, and what was happening in Love Canal became national news. The pressure of such media exposure forced the New York State Department of Health to act. After testing homes and soil nearest to the school, on August 2, 1978, the agency closed the school and ordered pregnant women and children under two to evacuate. However, the agency provided no aid, financial or otherwise, to facilitate the move. Predictably, those residents who did not fit the initial profile for evacuation began to fear the worst.

They were essentially being told to ride it out in an area poisoned by chemical waste that they had no idea existed beneath their homes and school.

The continued bad press finally forced the governor to order the full evacuation of 239 homes on or around the landfill. Furthermore, the state government committed to the purchase of those homes and to begin a major cleanup project in order to mitigate the disaster. President Jimmy Carter then signed off on federal emergency aid to the area, a process that up until then had been reserved only for natural disasters.

Eventually, officials expanded the infected area to include more homes. In 1980, President Carter ordered further federal aid that funded the relocation of any Love Canal resident who wished to leave. All told, the government spent over $60 million on the Love Canal disaster. A federal lawsuit forced Occidental Chemical (formerly Hooker Chemical) to reimburse the government for that amount.

The Love Canal evacuation and subsequent cleanup became the impetus for the creation of the Environmental Protection Agency Superfund. This program, started in 1980, empowers the EPA to identify hazardous waste sites and force those responsible to clean them up. It also provides funding when responsible parties are not identified or when money is needed. Critics contend today that the Superfund is so backlogged on cases and so short of funds that it has become ineffective.

The Love Canal neighborhood today is quite different from the one that existed prior to the evacuation. The area where the school and surrounding houses once stood is fenced off. The part of the neighborhood nearest the site contains empty lots lining empty streets. Further away, some houses still stand. While new houses cannot be built, some of the original owners chose to stay, their homes now reminders of the once-vibrant working-class neighborhood that was destroyed by a chemical time bomb put in place by a long-departed chemical company.

*In the End, we will remember not the
words of our enemies, but the silence
of our friends.*

Martin Luther King, Jr.

Act VIII

A young African-American minister steps outside his church after a Sunday service. It is a sunny and warm spring morning, perfect in every way, the kind of day Southerners brag about to their friends from the North. As the young preacher heads out for a walk to unwind between services, he is met by a group of young men from his church who are seeking his counsel. He invites the young men to join him on his walk.

Dialogue

◆ *Reverend, we are frustrated by the slow pace of change. We are tired of being victims. The racism that we face seems only to grow stronger and more prevalent every day. You speak of peaceful resistance, but those who hate us bring violence. How do we counter such injustice?*

✪ *Ours is a righteous battle. Stand tall with all your brothers and sisters who feel the pain of injustice. By doing so, you can change the hearts and minds of others. Carrying around hate in your heart puts your enemies in control. Responding to violence with more violence means that you have allowed those who hate you to change who you are. It is through peaceful resistance that we can best effect change.*

♦ *Do you really believe we can change the hearts of those who spit in our faces and call us names when we walk down the street? Can we change the hearts of those who set fire to our businesses and burn crosses on our lawns?*

Those who have such hate in their hearts may never change. It is the hearts and minds of the silent bystanders that we must reach. And that can only be accomplished through peace and love.

♦ *What is the most important thing we can do to help our cause?*

You know the pain of injustice. Use the example of the Lord and stand together—not only with one another, but also with others who are suffering—the poor, the hungry, the homeless, the dying—and share their pain. Such solidarity is the best weapon against violence. If you are a passive witness to any injustice, you cannot be true to our cause. For in the End, we will remember not the words of our enemies, but the silence of our friends.

A Simple Act

Sometimes care for others is expressed through the simplest of gestures. And the accretion of many small gestures, many small acts of compassion, can literally change the world. Most of us are not prepared to follow the example of Fr. Damien or Harriet Tubman and drop everything, leave our homes and our families, and commit to a life of service to a people we do not really know. But we can look around our own piece of the world and seek out those who need our care. And sometimes that care can be a simple act . . . like putting an arm around someone in need of some support.

The story of Jackie Robinson is well documented. His strength of character allowed him to stand tall in the midst of hatred and bigotry. Branch Rickey, president and general manager of the Brooklyn Dodgers, picked Jackie Robinson to break the color barrier in major league baseball. After a very lengthy interview, Rickey famously told Robinson that he needed a player with "guts enough not to fight back" when confronted with the inevitable racial slurs and discrimination that would come his way, someone who could handle the isolation of being an outsider in a game that is known for its tightly knit clubhouses and visible camaraderie. Robinson agreed to be that player, and in April of 1947 he became the first African-American player in the major leagues, starting at first base for the Brooklyn Dodgers.

His presence immediately caused a rift in the Dodgers clubhouse. Before spring training even began, several teammates, most of them Southerners, circulated a petition saying that they would refuse to play on the same field as Robinson. However, the popular leader of the team, shortstop Pee Wee Reese, himself a Southerner from Kentucky, refused to sign the petition. Reese saw Robinson not as a black man, but as a ballplayer, and stood up to his teammates when it would have been much easier to keep quiet or side with the majority. His courage quickly ended the rift and the Dodgers left spring training as a united team.

But the worst for Robinson lay ahead. The verbal abuse, taunts, racial slurs, and physical intimidation aimed at him by opposing teams and fans were relentless. All the while, Robinson knew he had to keep his word and not fight back if the "great experiment" was to succeed. He also understood that he would likely have to stand alone when facing such racism.

Nowhere was the abuse more pointed and personal than in Cincinnati. During the Dodgers' first trip to play the Reds, the heckling and racial insults by fans and opposing players were enough to break any man, especially one forced to stand alone. As the taunts reached their peak during infield practice, Pee Wee Reese walked over from his position at shortstop and put his arm around Jackie Robinson and the two men simply talked, seemingly oblivious to the hate that surrounded them. Here was a Southern white man standing arm in arm with a black teammate as they endured the taunts and insults of the fans and players together. They were telling the world that Robinson no longer stood alone, a simple act that helped change not only baseball, but the nation itself.

This image of Reese with his arm around Robinson is now immortalized by a bronze statue that stands in Brooklyn.

The Genovese Syndrome

Most everyone is familiar with the parable of the Good Samaritan. For most of us, after we read or hear the story, the natural reaction is to convince ourselves that placed in such a situation, we would act as the Samaritan did and offer aid and comfort to the beaten and injured stranger left by thieves to die on the side of the road. We read or hear of the behavior of the priest and Levite, who both cross to the other side of the road and leave the man for dead, and assure ourselves that we could never act in such a cruel and selfish manner.

But are we being honest? If we came upon a stranger in need, would we choose the inconvenience of action, or the convenience of silence?

On the morning of April 18, 2010, along a busy sidewalk in Queens, New York, Hugo Alfreo Tale-Yax, a homeless Guatemalan immigrant, observed a woman being threatened by a knife-wielding man. Hugo attempted to shield the woman and was stabbed multiple times by the attacker, who then ran off. Hugo attempted to pursue the man but collapsed to the sidewalk, bleeding from the multiple stab wounds. The woman who was being threatened also fled the scene.

It is what happened next that is most disturbing. A nearby security camera captured pedestrians, one by one, walking right past and even over Hugo as he lay on the sidewalk dying in a pool of his own blood. One man stopped and pulled out his phone. But instead of calling for help, he snapped a picture of the dying man on the sidewalk and left. Another man stopped and rolled him over, but then departed without doing anything. For well over an hour people walked by Hugo, most without even acknowledging his presence, none willing to stop and offer aid. Finally, someone apparently called for an ambulance and help arrived. But it was too late; Hugo was dead. He had acted as a Good Samaritan and come to the aid of a stranger, and his reward was to be left to die on the sidewalk as busy New Yorkers rushed right by him and went on with their day.

Why did so many people walk right by the dying man without even calling for help? Maybe Hugo's unkempt and haggard appearance played into the attitude of the passersby. Perhaps they were used to seeing homeless on the street and may have thought he was merely drunk. But that does not explain the behavior of the man with the camera or the man who rolled him over. And someone must have seen him fall after being stabbed. Certainly others must have seen the pool of blood.

Maybe the bystanders were merely assuming someone else would take the time to call for help or aid the dying man. Or maybe these busy New Yorkers paraded right by simply because they were unwilling to interrupt their own hectic schedule on account of something they had nothing to do with, involving someone they did not know.

The silence of bystanders also played a part in another famous crime that occurred on a New York street decades before. In the early hours of March 13, 1964, twenty-nine-year-old Kitty Genovese returned home from her job as a bar manager. She parked her car and walked across the street to her Queens apartment building. A complete stranger, who later admitted he was out seeking a vulnerable woman to kill, attacked and stabbed her in the street. She screamed and cried out for help. The man ran off when someone yelled out a window. Kitty staggered to the back of the building, but was unable to get in.

Witnesses would later say that the man left in a car, but returned after about ten minutes. He found Kitty lying in the door at the back of the building and proceeded to stab her and rape her on the spot. She fought back and screamed with the energy that she had left. But no one came to her aid, and she died outside the door of her apartment building.

There was much debate about who saw or heard what. The *New York Times* wrote a misleading piece entitled "38 Who Saw Murder Didn't Call the Police," further sensationalizing the role of the witnesses. What is clear is that there were witnesses to the initial attack and other witnesses who saw the man return. It is also clear that several residents in the building heard the screams and cries for help as Kitty was being attacked and raped, and it was not until well after that final attack that one of them finally called the police.

The immediate reaction to the silence of the witnesses in her building was one of outrage, partially fueled by the *Times* article, but mostly the result of people wanting to believe that they would never have behaved with such indifference, that they would have stepped forward and come to the aid of the victim.

The long-term reaction focused more on the social and psychological forces at work among the witnesses. In fact, the bystander apathy described in the case became known as the Genovese Syndrome. Psychologists point to a diffusion of responsibility that occurs among bystanders and witnesses. The larger the crowd, the easier it is for a single bystander to stay silent when someone is in distress. So, ironically enough, if you are a victim needing help, your best bet to be noticed is for a single bystander to happen by. The last thing you need is for a crowd to show up!

Of course, this Genovese Syndrome cannot be an excuse for the witnesses who shut their windows as Kitty Genovese screamed. Nor can it excuse a people stepping over a dying man on a sidewalk. And it certainly cannot excuse someone taking a picture of the dying man and then walking away. Such indifference to the plight of another human being can only be described as cold and callous, the Good Samaritan turned upside down.

Separated by four decades, for both these victims of crimes on the streets of New York, the silence of neighbors and bystanders proved fatal.

*You never really understand a person . . .
until you climb into his skin and walk
around in it.*

Atticus Finch, <u>To Kill a Mockingbird</u>
Harper Lee

Act IX

A tall, lanky man in a fedora and a well-worn light-colored suit holds the hand of his precocious tomboy daughter as she skips along beside him in her overalls and faded sneakers. They are headed home as dusk nears on a warm summer evening in a sleepy Southern town. The girl has a quizzical look on her face as she looks up at father.

Dialogue

♦ *Somethin' I don't get. Why do people seem to care so much about what color a man's skin is? Seems like a silly thing to be concerned about. Why don't they care as much about the color of his hair or eyes?*

I wish I had an answer to that question.

♦ *To hate somebody just 'cause they don't look or talk or act like you, that's pretty stupid.*

We all fear that which is different or new or makes us uncomfortable. Human nature leads us to view ourselves as the

135

center of the world. Accepting something or someone that is new or different is a threat to the attention we crave, the control we desire.

♦ *So everybody runs around lookin' at the world one way, never thinkin' at all that someone else might see the same thing they lookin' at a little different?*

Our greatest fear is to be inconsequential. Too many people think that they can have a meaningful, noteworthy existence only at the expense of someone else. In other words, to validate their own lives, they need to tear down the lives of others. And those others usually look or talk or act differently than they do.

♦ *So how is that ever gonna change?*

Well, you can start with yourself and see how that goes. Whenever you catch yourself feeling superior, stop and remember that your view of the world is not the only one and others might see things a bit differently. And before you judge the way others see the world, before you dismiss their way of looking at things, stand for a moment in their shoes. You never really understand a person until you climb into his skin and walk around in it.

The Same God Made Both of Us

If, only for a moment, we could walk in their moccasins. How else can we really appreciate the indignity and suffering endured by Native Americans during the westward expansion of the United State in the nineteenth century? Of course, we cannot really walk the path of another people from another time. But we do have an obligation to try to understand what happened to the many great and proud Native American tribes who lived on this land long before the arrival of white settlers. The story of a Ponca Chief named Standing Bear illustrates the terrible injustices carried out by the United States government against a native people whom it viewed as an inconvenient obstacle to the Manifest Destiny of a nation. The story also reveals the strong character and resilience of the people who stood tall and proud in the face of such hardship and persecution.

By the time of the first contact with Europeans in the New World, the Ponca Tribe had settled along the Niobrara River in northeastern Nebraska. As a small tribe (the population had shrunk to around 200 by the time of the Lewis and Clark Expedition due to a smallpox epidemic), they sustained themselves by growing corn and other crops in the summer and hunting bison in the winter. This lifestyle required following the buffalo herds, making them a partially nomadic people. Such an existence brought them into contact and conflict with other tribes in the area, such as the Oglala Sioux and the Pawnee. Raids and counter-raids became a way of life.

The Kansas-Nebraska Act of 1854 expedited the movement of white settlers into the Ponca territory. These new settlers began to pressure the government to do something about the "Indian problem" that was impeding what they viewed as their rightful claim to the land. Tribes such as the Ponca who had settled and been stewards of these lands for generations became roadblocks as America expanded westward. With so many white settlers demanding land, the government needed to revise its Indian policy which, up to that time, had focused on minimizing interaction between the Native American tribes and the white settlers. In order to solve the "Indian problem," the government established a new policy of tribal relocation from the desirable land of the Great Plains to specially designated Indian Territories.

The issue of the Ponca Tribe became a case study in government exploitation and abuse of a peaceful and prosperous people. A one-sided treaty with the government led the tribe to move to a less desirable location nearby that was not well-suited for crops and hunting. The story could have ended here with the Ponca making the best of their new homeland and continuing their way of life, but the government managed to further screw things up. As part of a larger land treaty, the Bureau of Indian Affairs inadvertently included the land the Ponca Tribe now resided on as part of a larger land treaty with the Sioux. Obviously, the presence of the Ponca on what was now Sioux land created conflict and the Ponca suffered greatly as a result of the constant raids that ensued.

The solution that the government came up with to rectify its mistake was to relocate the Ponca Tribe once again, only this time to Indian Territory in present-day Oklahoma. Agents of the Bureau of Indian Affairs met with several Ponca chiefs, including Standing Bear, and coaxed them into signing a letter agreeing to cede all Ponca lands in the Nebraska Territory and relocate to a supposedly similar tract of land in Indian Territory. The chiefs later said they had been misinformed and thought they had agreed to move to the Omaha Reservation in eastern Nebraska.

As far back as Thomas Jefferson, government leaders had sought to create a colony for an Indian population that, in their eyes, stood in the way of the natural expansion of the country. Andrew Jackson conceived of Indian Territory as the area west of the Mississippi. But soon it became apparent that the northern plains held fertile land suitable for settlement, so Indian Territory shrank in size and eventually was confined to part of present-day Oklahoma. The area was not really a territory and had only an informal existence at its inception. But, out of necessity, the federal government eventually exerted control.

In 1877, the process of forcing the Ponca people from their homeland began. A tribal delegation that included Standing Bear and other tribal chiefs accompanied a government official to Oklahoma to find suitable land. Representatives of the government insisted that the Oklahoma territory had many locations that would be even more bountiful than the land along the Niobrara. Of course, when the delegation arrived in Oklahoma, they found a desolate terrain. The area was unsuitable for the Ponca to resume a way of life sustained by hunting and farming. The Ponca chiefs were upset that they had been misled by the government into believing that Indian Territory would be a bountiful land.

Of course, the government official who had brought them there saw things differently and accused the tribal chiefs of being disrespectful and incorrigible. He abandoned them in Oklahoma and refused to aid them in their return. So, in the middle of winter, with no supplies, the tribal delegation walked the 500 miles back home, sleeping on the prairie and living off the land. It took fifty days.

The government would get its way. The forced relocation of the Ponca soon began. Eventually the entire tribe made the slow and arduous trek to a tract of land in the Indian Territory designated as their new homeland. The suffering of the Ponca only intensified once they arrived. Crops failed, livestock could not be sustained, and hunting was limited. Hunger and disease became the new enemy and a sizeable portion of the tribe was wiped out in those first few years in the new land. This once self-sufficient people who had acted as caretakers of the land and of the massive buffalo herds of the northern plains had been reduced to a dying tribe held prisoner in a faraway land, with no resources and no hope.

One of the casualties of the wave of disease that struck the tribe was the son of Chief Standing Bear. When the boy fell ill, he made his father promise to bury him in the rightful homeland of the Ponca. Standing Bear gave his word and when the boy died, he made the decision to return to his homeland at the mouth of the Niobrara River to bury his son and reclaim the existence that had been stolen from his people.

Accompanied by a significant delegation from the tribe, Standing Bear loaded up the remains of his dead son on a cart and began what would be a ten-week journey in the dead of winter. Of course, the sight of this long procession of Native Americans moving north out of Indian Territory alarmed the white settlers who had taken over the land in Kansas and Nebraska.

Standing Bear eventually led the delegation into the land of the Omaha Tribe, who shared their language and were their allies. However, the United States cavalry soon arrived and arrested the delegation on the grounds that they had violated an order of the federal government by leaving the reservation. General George Crook of Fort Omaha ordered the arrest but, as a veteran of many military campaigns and treaties involving tribes throughout the West, he was sympathetic to the plight of Standing Bear and his people. In fact, it is almost certain that Crook himself encouraged Thomas Tibbles, a crusading newspaper editor at the Omaha *Daily Herald*, to take up the cause of Standing Bear and rally public support.

Soon two prominent Omaha attorneys, John Webster and Andrew Poppleton, agreed to represent Standing Bear and filed a suit against the government on his behalf. Citing the Fourteenth Amendment, they claimed that Standing Bear's rights had been violated and he had been illegally detained. A Native American was, for the first time, claiming citizenship along with all its inherent privileges, rights, and freedoms.

And, to the surprise of many (including the Bureau of Indian Affairs), Judge Elmer Dundy ruled in favor of Standing Bear. The precedent had been set: Native Americans were entitled to the same rights as the white settlers who, with the aid of the federal government, had taken their land. Such a ruling certainly would cause inconvenience to those who profited from the push west. After all, the "Indian problem" had supposedly been solved by the policy of claiming land and displacing the pesky native people to an out-of-the-way reservation. Denying the humanity of these proud people had always been an expedient way of justifying government Indian policy. Standing Bear famously addressed this notion when he made the following plea to Judge Dundy: "My hand is not the color of yours, but if I pierce it, I shall feel pain. The blood that will flow from mine will be of the same color as yours. I am a man. The same God made both of us."

Though the ruling in the case of Standing Bear had been clear, the concept of treating Native Americans as citizens rather than savages did not immediately affect the Indian policy of the government. However, the Ponca Tribe benefitted from the strong public sentiment for Standing Bear and his plight (thanks in part to Tibbles and his reporting in the *Daily Herald*). The government set up a reservation along the Niobrara River for the Ponca. Thus, members of the tribe today can be found both in northeast Nebraska and Oklahoma.

If only we all could just once walk in the moccasins of Standing Bear. Then we might appreciate the incredible strength and dignity that sustained him and his people through persecution and suffering carried out by a government that denied their very humanity.

Executive Order 9066

We all take pride in our ancestry. Where we come from influences who we are and who we will become. It even determines what we look like. But for Americans of Japanese heritage at the start of World War II, ancestry meant being branded an enemy.

The unwarranted distrust of and outright contempt for Japanese-Americans that reached its peak just after the bombing of Pearl Harbor had been brewing throughout the first half of the century. Japanese workers entered the labor market in earnest in the late 1800s and by the turn of the century competition for jobs, especially in the farming areas of the West Coast, caused friction between white laborers and the Japanese workers perceived to be taking their jobs. Discriminatory laws led to segregation of the Japanese population and made life tough for these first and second-generation immigrants from the Far East.

December 7, 1941 changed everything. The United States was at war. The public distrust of Japanese-Americans became even more pronounced. Rumors about spies and an imminent Japanese invasion of the mainland quickly spread. Politicians and civic leaders took up the cause of safeguarding the West Coast from the Japanese enemy. General John DeWitt of the Army's Western Command sought to remove all "enemy aliens" from the coast and proceeded to formulate a relocation policy with the backing of none other than George Marshall, the chief military advisor of President Franklin Roosevelt. Eventually, the White House released a letter outlining the right of the government in wartime to mass evacuate any group of people determined to be a threat to national security. President Roosevelt then signed Executive Order 9066 on February 19, 1942, empowering the government to forcibly remove anyone of Japanese ancestry to government internment camps. So from that day forward during the war, having the wrong ancestry and wrong skin color would be enough to cause those of Japanese ancestry to lose their homes and their freedom.

The establishment of the evacuation policy and creation of the War Relocation Authority (WRA) was the first step in the forced internment of 120,000 men, women, and children of Japanese ancestry along the West Coast. Over two-thirds were American citizens. The process for rounding up and evacuating the Japanese-Americans was swift and callous. Those targeted for internment were allowed to bring only a limited number of belongings. Most had no prior notice of being evacuated and no idea where they would be going. As a result, they had to quickly board up their businesses and homes and sell their possessions. Con artists moved in and ripped off many of these victims by offering to buy these possessions at well below market value. In many cases, the government officials split up families. And often these families would not be reunited for nearly four years.

The evacuees boarded trains and headed to one of the ten WRA internment camps spread throughout the Western states. These camps were situated in remote locations, many in desert settings. Surrounded by barbed-wire fencing and manned by armed guards, these camps consisted of simple army-style barracks. Plumbing was limited or, in some camps, not available at all. Fresh water and food were rationed. The extreme settings of the camps, with unbearably hot days and cold nights, heightened the misery. Inadequate medical care affected especially the children and the elderly who populated the camps.

In essence, Japanese-Americans became prisoners in their own country, incarcerated by their own government. In a further effort to roust out any prisoners who maintained a loyalty to the Japanese government, camp officials required everyone in the camps to complete a loyalty questionnaire. Officials then sent any prisoners deemed disloyal because of answers on the questionnaire to a high-security camp at Tule Lake in California.

In 1944, the government made interred Japanese-American males of appropriate age draft-eligible. So young Japanese-Americans being held in a wartime prison were now eligible to fight for the country that had put them there without cause in the first place. Over 26,000 Japanese-Americans eventually served in World War II, including the 442nd Regimental Combat Team and the 100th Infantry Battalion, which were nearly completely comprised of Japanese-Americans.

Several court challenges to the internment process would occur over the course of the war. But it was a suit filed by a civil servant worker in California that eventually led to the end of the internment camp nightmare for Japanese-Americans. Mitsuye Endo lost her government job in Sacramento during the evacuation hysteria. She was then told to report to an internment camp. She challenged the right of the government to take such action and her lawyer filed a writ of habeas corpus. The government, hoping to avoid a test of the Executive Order in court, offered to simply relocate Ms. Endo to another state. She refused so that her case would proceed.

The case made it to the Supreme Court, which in December of 1944 ruled in her favor, essentially declaring the internment process unconstitutional despite the ongoing war. Just prior to the decision, the government, aware that the Court was about to deliver a decision that would prove embarrassing to the White House, terminated the

Executive Order and began to close the WRA camps. The process was slow, but most interred prisoners went home by December of 1945. The last camp to close was Tule Lake in March of 1946.

Being released from an internment camp was one thing. Regaining a stolen life was another. Forced to abandon everything prior to evacuation, most of those who spent the war years as prisoners returned home to nothing. Homes and businesses that did survive had either been vandalized or had fallen into disrepair. Post-war resentment fueled further discrimination, especially in the West. The Japanese communities in San Francisco and Los Angeles would never return to their pre-war vibrancy. But despite these obstacles, over time, through perseverance and hard work, many Japanese-Americans slowly rebuilt their lives.

The government that was so swift in carrying out the relocation order during the war was very slow to rectify the injustice done to the Japanese-American victims and their families. It was not until 1988 that the government finally offered an official apology and reparations to the victims of Executive Order 9066.

Incidentally, during the war only ten people were convicted of spying for Japan. All ten were white.

Everything can be taken from a man but one thing: the last of the human freedoms—to choose one's attitude in any given set of circumstances, to choose one's own way.

Viktor Frankl

Act X

Wearing a long, dark overcoat and scarf to shield himself from the blustery wind and light rain, an old man leans on his grandson, a tall, dark-haired young man in his late twenties, who is neatly dressed in a suit but also shielded from the weather by a warm overcoat. The two are standing before the gate at Auschwitz, a half century after the unspeakable atrocities that occurred there, atrocities that the old man experienced firsthand.

Dialogue

✡ *The unthinkable occurred inside this gate. You must see this place so that you and your generation never allow it to happen again. In this camp, I watched men commit unimaginable acts against defenseless people. I saw it all happen; you must at least see where it happened.*

♦ *Tell me what you felt when you first entered this gate.*

✡ *We were brought here by train like animals, crowded into cattle cars. The heat was unbearable as we stood motionless in the* cars, covered in dirt and sweat with no food or water, a single bucket for a latrine. We learned later that when the train stopped, many of the prisoners were marched straight to the gas chamber. The rest of us were herded off the train and processed. All of our clothes and belongings were taken and we were shaved and tattooed with the number that would be our identity.

♦ *What is that written above the gate?*

✡ *"Arbeit Macht Frei"—Work makes one free. What irony. We were slaves who were worked until we were no longer useful and then sent to die in a gas chamber. Each day we would leave the Block, after spending the night crammed together into a rat-infested room with an intolerable stench, all of us sick and emaciated, and march out this gate to the labor camps. Right there, inside the gate, the Nazis would have a band playing German songs as we marched. But this place was hell no matter how much music was played or what was written on the gate. One and a half million men, women, and children were murdered inside this gate.*

♦ *What kept you going? You must have given up hope at some point.*

✡ *I was stripped of my family, my possessions, my health, food and water, even my name. I was beaten and subjected to psychological abuse; I was forced to witness unspeakable acts of torture carried out on my fellow Jews. The Nazis stripped me of everything except for the one thing they could not touch: my spirit. Everything can be taken from a man but one thing: the last of the human freedoms—to choose one's attitude in any given set of circumstances, to choose one's own way. Now come and let me show you this place so you may be a witness when I am gone.*

Survivors

The first tank from the U.S. Third Army rolled up to the gate of Buchenwald on April 11, 1945. The concentration camp was now liberated. A seventeen-year-old emaciated and starving boy who had witnessed unspeakable evil and endured torture, forced labor and endless marches, was among those who survived. The boy would become a man and he would later write that at the point of freedom hunger trumped all other feelings—revenge, hatred, and sorrow would have to wait. Days later, after the boy had fought off illness, he stood in front of a mirror and saw a corpse of a man staring back. Elie Wiesel then began to process the hell he had survived . . .

A young Jewish doctor, who had been separated from his family and moved from one concentration camp to another, was now at Turkheim working as a slave laborer. After three and a half years in these camps, he was starving, sick with typhoid, and desperate to stay awake so as to avoid the infirmary, which meant certain death. Fighting off disillusionment and searching for meaning even in the suffering he endured, the young doctor was holding on. It was then that the Americans rolled into camp and liberated the survivors of Turkheim, including Dr. Viktor Frankl . . .

Two men stripped of everything, subjected to an indescribable existence, witness to unimaginable evil. What kept them going amidst the pain and suffering, the torture, the starvation, the psychological torment? Why did they survive?

Elie Wiesel was born and raised in Sighet, Romania, along with his older sisters Hilda and Beatrice and his younger sister Tzipora. His father and mother spoke Yiddish at home and their Jewish faith was the focus of their family life. Encouraged by his parents, Elie spent much of his time studying the Torah.

In 1944, when Wiesel was sixteen years old, the war reached Sighet. Hungarian officials, who were in control of the town, rounded up the Jewish families of the town and relocated them to designated ghettos. Though they were herded into a prison-like existence, there was no panic, for the prevailing wisdom was that the front was moving closer and the war would soon end. Despite reports of atrocities committed against Jews by the Nazis elsewhere, there was a feeling in the ghetto that the Jews of Sighet would be spared.

Then the first German officers appeared and rumors spread about their intentions, creating a sense of hysteria. Eventually, the Jews of Sighet, among them Wiesel and his family, were ordered to prepare for deportation. In large groups, they were stripped of their possessions, marched to the train tracks outside of town, and placed in overcrowded cattle cars. The trains departed for a destination unknown to the Jewish prisoners. The journey was torturous as the men, women, and children prisoners endured unbearable thirst and hunger, the smell of urine, inescapable heat, and overcrowding that left them nowhere to move and no room to sit down.

Yet, even such unbearable conditions would pale in comparison to what was to come.

Upon arrival at the camp, the guards ordered them off the train and they faced the first selection, a process of separating out those prisoners that the panel of officers and doctors deemed unfit. Wiesel described the first selection in his book *Night*:

> *Men to the left! Women to the right! Eight words*
> *spoken without emotion . . . I didn't know this was the*
> *time and place I was leaving my mother and (sister)*
> *Tzapia forever . . .*

He would later learn that his mother and sister had been marched off the train straight to the crematorium.

It would now be Wiesel's sole objective to stay by his father's side. Together they would endure the harsh realities of the concentration camp, the physical and psychological torture carried out by evil men in an evil place. And together they would witness atrocities no one thought possible: children being thrown into a fiery ditch, left to burn to death; the constant smoke emerging from the crematorium; fellow Jews starving to death, wrought with dysentery and other disease, beaten to a pulp by sadistic Nazi guards; a child hanged in the gallows in the yard and left to die a slow agonizing death because he was too light for his neck to break; prisoners shot in the back for sport to entertain bored guards and officers.

And each time they were lined up for another selection, father and son managed to remain alive together, passing through the inspection by the Nazi doctors and officers and ending up in the chosen group.

Then one day Nazis ordered the prisoners to prepare to evacuate. They were forced to march in the freezing snow, with no food or water. On occasion the guards ordered them to run. Many prisoners dropped to the ground, weakened by exhaustion, and ended up trampled to death in the snow.

Wiesel and his father fought off the urge to give up. Together they found the resolve to survive this death march. Eventually the prisoners that were left arrived at Buchenwald, a camp further from the advancing front. Wiesel's father soon became sick there. The other prisoners, desperate to survive, turned on him in the barracks, even stealing his rations. His father weakened. Wiesel described the end:

> *In my father's cot lay another sick person . . . No prayers were said over his tomb. No candle lit in his memory. His last word had been my name. He had called out to me and I had not answered. I did not weep, and it pained me that I could not weep. But I was out of tears.*

The U.S. Third Army tank appeared at the Buchenwald gate four months later.

A similar fate would befall Viktor Frankl, who was a well known psychiatrist and neurologist in Vienna at the time of the Nazi occupation of Austria in 1938. He had established himself as a leading scholar and practitioner in the field of psychology, following in the footsteps of Freud, Adler, and others of the famed Viennese Psychoanalytic Society. After the Nazi takeover, Frankl began work at the only hospital in Vienna that would treat Jews. He worked tirelessly to protect his patients from the Nazi euthanasia policy for those with mental illness, often by providing misdiagnoses.

In 1942, Frankl and his family were sent to the Theresienstadt concentration camp, where they were split up. Most of Frankl's family did not survive the camps. He would eventually learn their fate: his wife died in the gas chamber at Bergen-Belsen, his father died of starvation at Thersienstadt, and his mother was murdered at Auschwitz.

Frankl's experiences included moves from Theresienstadt to Auschwitz to Turkheim. He endured the harsh realities of life as a slave laborer at these camps: sleep deprivation, near-starvation, intolerable living conditions, long hours of mindless manual labor, forced marches in bitter cold conditions. It was during these long marches to the work sites that Frankl began to realize why some men survived the horrors of the camp while others simply gave up. As they marched, driven along like animals by the cruel Nazi guards, Frankl began to retreat from the horror by turning to thoughts of his wife. Even in the most desperate circumstances, he found meaning in the contemplation of his love for her. He imagined that the other prisoners were also lost in such thoughts as they quietly endured the long marches. These men had one freedom left: spiritual freedom. And they found it even amidst the evil of the concentration camp. Frankl writes of this freedom in his book *Man's Search for Meaning:*

We who lived in concentration camps can remember the men who walked through the huts comforting others, giving away their last piece of bread . . . . Every day, every hour, offered the opportunity to make a decision, a decision whether you would or would not submit to those powers which threatened to rob you of your very self, your inner freedom . . .

Those who survived found meaning even in the suffering. Frankl saw men bear indescribable physical and psychological abuse in the camps and he believed their strength came from retreating to an inner spiritual sanctuary, a place out of reach of the sadistic Nazi guards. Avoiding a loss of meaning in life (Frankl called it the existential vacuum) was essential if prisoners faced with such constant persecution were to survive. In such an environment, that meaning could be found only internally, by reflecting on the love of God and family.

After being moved from Auschwitz to Turkheim, Frankl worked as a slave laborer while suffering from typhoid. Six months after he arrived at the camp, the American forces liberated Turkheim and he was free.

Elie Wiesel and Viktor Frankl.

Victims. Witnesses. Survivors.

Stripped of everything.

Except their spiritual freedom and dignity.

I Promise

The story goes that one December morning in a small town in Armenia, a father walked his young son to school. He made this walk with his son every morning, savoring the time they could spend together before he went to work. When they reached the schoolyard the father kissed his son goodbye and, as he did at the end of every morning walk, said to him, "Son, I love you and I promise I will come back to get you!"

The father then watched as his son, with his book bag in tow, walked into school. The father turned and headed to work.

Right before the noon hour, the earth shook. What would be known as the great Spitak earthquake struck the Armenian town that December day in 1988, measuring 6.9 on the Richter scale. The town was leveled. At the time, Armenia was still part of the Soviet Union and the town had been poorly constructed with substandard materials. Over 25,000 people lost their lives in the destruction, their bodies buried in the rubble.

The father, who survived the quake, rushed back to the school only to find a pile of rock where it once stood. The earthquake had destroyed the entire school, the building collapsing on the teachers and children inside. Parents and relatives stood by helpless, frozen by grief for the children they lost that day.

Without hesitation, the father ran to the destroyed school building and, using his bare hands, began to dig. One by one, he pulled away pieces of debris and blocks of cement. An hour went by. Others came by and urged him to give up, for there was no hope: "They are all gone. Show some sense. Your son is dead." The man continued to dig, his hands bloodied from the sharp rocks and metal. Eight hours with no sign of hope. He continued on. Night fell and dawn came, and the father still refused to give up. By now, bystanders thought he had lost his mind: "He must be mad. The quake left behind only death and destruction." He just kept digging. Time passed. Exhausted, he kept moving rocks. People now even began to mock him. "This man is a fool."

He continued to dig. Then, many hours after he started, the father moved aside a stone and there staring up at him was his son. A smile came across his son's face as he cried out, "Dad!"

And then the boy turned and called back to the dozen other kids trapped with him and said, "See, I told you my dad promised he would come back and get me."

A father who, despite what others did or said, never gave up, driven solely by his love for his son.

A son who, knowing how much his father loved him, never gave up, providing comfort and hope to the others trapped with him.

Gulag

The son of Polish immigrants, Walter Ciszek grew up in a small Pennsylvania town in the early 1900s. He was, by his own account, a rather wild young man who was known to engage in a brawl now and again. His untamed nature made his decision to become a priest quite surprising to those who knew him. Nonetheless, Ciszek entered the Jesuit novitiate in upstate New York in 1928. While discerning his future, he heard Pope Pius XI call for Jesuits to do mission work in Russia, where Stalin had all but destroyed the Russian Orthodox Church. Ciszek saw this "Russian Mission" as his calling. He was ordained in 1937.

Since at the time no one was entering Russia, Ciszek took a post in Albertyn, Poland, where he taught at the novitiate and ministered to the local people. Eventually, the war came to eastern Poland, and as the Nazis invaded from the west, the Russians came from the east. Albertyn was taken over by the Red Army in 1939. The church was ransacked and the Jesuit College occupied. While others fled the area, Ciszek remained and saw an opportunity to realize his dream of entering Russia. He and another Jesuit priest lost themselves among the many refugees that were now wandering the area.

Having received permission from his superior to seek a way into Russia, Ciszek and his companion assumed new identities and got hired, along with other refugees, to work in Russia. Ciszek ended up hauling logs at a large lumber outfit in the Ural Mountains. His ministry became the hard labor of a logging camp employee. He also managed to sneak into the woods regularly to pray and offer mass. The life of a logger certainly took its toll but Ciszek, driven by a passion for doing the will of God, embraced his new life in Russia, regardless of the toils that he had to endure.

Then everything changed one summer evening when the secret police showed up at Ciszek's bunkhouse. They searched his bunk, confiscated his belongings, and then arrested him. He was eventually taken to Perm and put in a thirty-by-thirty-foot cell with over one hundred other prisoners. He learned from others that the German invasion of the Soviet Union had led the secret police to begin arresting those who aroused suspicion. Because of the growing paranoia of the communist government, anyone could be whisked away from his home without warning, sometimes never to be seen again. The government had set up a series of secret prisons and labor camps to deal with those who were perceived as a threat to the government. Eventually, millions of people would end up in this secret prison system known as the Gulag.

At Perm, Ciszek underwent the first of countless interrogations. These occurred at all hours and included physical and psychological abuse. It was during one of the early interrogations that Ciszek realized his real identity had been found out. The officials revealed that they knew he was a priest named Ciszek who had entered the country illegally. He would never learn how he had been discovered.

After a few months, Ciszek was taken by train to Moscow and sent to the infamous Lubianka prison. Here he was subjected to solitary confinement, more interrogations, and regular physical and psychological abuse. He was given little to eat or drink. Through it all, Ciszek believed his circumstances were part of God's plan. He continued to pray regularly and began to offer confession to other prisoners, finding his priestly calling in the most severe of surroundings.

After four years in Lubianka, Ciszek was convicted of espionage and sentenced to serve a sentence of fifteen years of hard labor in Siberia. The journey by train across Russia would have broken most men. He was jammed in a boxcar with dozens of other prisoners, including many hardened criminals, and endured a two-week trip with minimal food, no room to move, and no chance for any hygiene. He continued his habit of prayer and priestly duties during the passage to Siberia. After two weeks, the guards transferred the prisoners from the train to a barge, which took them to Norilsk, north of the Arctic Circle. Ciszek had left Moscow in the sweltering heat. He arrived in Norilsk in the frigid cold.

Even the unforgiving life he had endured in Moscow could not compare to what awaited Ciszek in the labor camp at Norilsk. He was housed with murderers, thieves, and rapists. His work assignments included loading coal on to barges, digging in the mines, and doing manual labor at construction sites, twelve hours per day, often in the freezing temperatures and blowing snow, wearing only prison-issue cotton clothes and broken shoes. Exhaustion, hunger, thirst, loneliness, and depression would eat at him. Yet he remained resolute in his conviction that he was following the will of God.

It was at Norilsk that Ciszek began to say mass for some of the Polish prisoners, using a makeshift chalice and whatever he could scrape up for bread and wine. He also resumed hearing confessions and even offering priestly counsel. Always careful to avoid detection by the guards, Ciszek spent most of his nights ministering to his fellow prisoners, helping them to find God in the seemingly hopeless life they led in a labor camp in Siberia. Days turned into weeks, weeks into months, and months into years. Ciszek was carrying out his Russian mission in a way he could never have imagined. Not even a sentence of hard labor in the Gulag had dampened his resolve to share his love of God with the Russian people.

In the spring of 1955, after fifteen years in the system, Ciszek was released from the labor camp; he was technically a "free" man. However, the secret police made it clear he could not leave the town of Norilsk. So he took work at a factory and began to perform his priestly duties for the townspeople. He celebrated mass, performed baptisms and weddings, and offered confession to the Catholic population. He was simply continuing his prison ministry in the town outside the labor camp gates. But his popularity as a priest aroused suspicion in the government, and Ciszek was eventually sent to another city closer to Moscow. Of course, he took up his mission among the people of that town and once again his ministry thrived and government officials once again became suspicious of his motives.

When he had been released from the Norilsk prison, Ciszek had obtained permission to write to his sisters in the United States. They had, of course, assumed he was dead, as they had not heard from him for twenty years. Ciszek received a letter back, but was not able to talk to or see them. That changed in 1963, when Soviet officials gave Ciszek over to the American consulate in Moscow as part of a prisoner swap initiated by the Kennedy Administration. Ciszek was headed back to the United States, a home he hardly knew.

Ciszek was reunited with his sisters. His Russian mission was complete. He had answered the call of Pope Pius XI to minister to the people of Russia. There is no way he could have imagined the life that he would lead in pursuit of that mission. Yet despite the pain, suffering, and despair he endured in the Gulag, Ciszek remained steadfast in his faith and maintained an attitude of thanksgiving as he carried out his ministry.

Captive, yet free.

Chikurubi

When the guards came into the cell and told Reon Schutte to put on his clothes and come with them, he assumed it meant another beating. Twelve years in the worst prison in the world had taught him that being singled out by the guards was the last thing a prisoner wanted. But this time the unexpected happened. The guards led him out the prison door, where he was handed over to a diplomat and, suddenly, he was a free man, thrust into a world he did not know, a world that had mostly forgotten him. Near death from disease and malnourishment, Reon had survived hell and would soon be able to share his story with the world. That story is a remarkable tale of how the power of choice can strengthen the mind and soul in even the most hopeless circumstances, and how forgiveness is what ultimately sets us free.

Reon is an Afrikaner, an ethnic group of white South Africans descended from the Dutch, German, and French groups that settled along the coast of present-day South Africa during the 1600s when the area served as a way station for those traders sailing around the Cape of Good Hope. Afrikaners eventually moved inland and became farmers (the Afrikaner word for farmer is *boer*). When gold was discovered in the late nineteenth century, Britain moved to annex the territories that had been claimed by the Afrikaners, resulting in the First and Second Boer Wars. The Afrikaners, or Boers, maintained their independence with victory in the first conflict. But the British returned with a more aggressive campaign in the Second Boer War and won a decisive victory that resulted in the territories being absorbed into the British Empire. It was not until 1961, the year Reon Schutte was born, that the white minority officially broke away from the British Commonwealth and formed the Republic of South Africa.

Reon came of age as the apartheid government took control of South Africa and consolidated its power. When he was sixteen, Reon joined the military. Because South Africa required two years of compulsory military service for all white males, Reon intended to meet his obligation and then return to civilian life. However, his exemplary service led his superiors to offer him a role in the elite South African Special Forces, and Reon became a career soldier involved in covert operations along the South African border. South Africa's relationships with the neighboring countries, especially Zimbabwe, were tense. The white supremacist regime in South Africa was literally in a constant state of high alert during this post-colonial era. Countless missions across borders and into hostile territories defined Reon's career throughout the 1980s.

But change was on the way in the South Africa. The country became increasingly isolated from the rest of the world, and the ruling class was being aggressively challenged internally by the resistance party known as the African National Congress (ANC). Amidst such pressures, the white ruling class in South Africa, led by

F.W. De Klerk, negotiated an end to apartheid with Nelson Mandela and the ANC in 1992, resulting in a peaceful transfer of power to a multinational government.

As a result of the political upheaval, military operations along the border ceased. At the time of the transition, Reon was involved in an operation in Zimbabwe. His last mission before being recalled involved rescuing some captured soldiers. Upon completion, he would head home with his comrades to the new South Africa.

Unfortunately, fate intervened and Reon would not see the new South Africa for a very long time. Things went awry on this last mission, and Reon ended up being arrested by Zimbabwe police. Government officials accused him of stealing a car and possessing a weapon. They also tagged him as a spy and an enemy combatant.

No help would come for Reon. The South African government disavowed knowledge of his presence in Zimbabwe and he was left to fend for himself. The government sentenced him to twenty-six years in the brutal and infamous Chikurubi Prison, considered the worst prison in the world by human rights organizations. A death sentence would be considered merciful compared to time in Chikurubi.

When he entered the prison in 1992, the imposing cement fortress housed 5000 prisoners and 2000 guards: Reon was the only white among them. That circumstance alone would change forever the world view of this South African soldier. Upon arrival, the guards stripped him and gave him the only three things Reon would possess for the next fourteen years: a dirty t-shirt, torn shorts, and a lice-infested blanket. He was immediately taken into the bowels of the prison through winding tunnels. Passing numerous windowless cells along the way, the guard finally stopped in front of a door and opened it. Inside the eight meter by twelve meter cell lay fifty other naked prisoners crammed together in a space designed for no more than twelve. The walls and floor were cement, and there was no outside light. The guards took off Reon's t-shirt and shorts and slammed the door.

It is, of course, impossible to accurately describe the inhumane circumstances that these prisoners endured, but Reon's account of his incarceration can give us at least some sense of the hellish existence that is still present at Chikurubi even today. Sleeping was next to impossible. The naked men lined up in rows practically on top of one another. Those closest to the wall had to curl up their legs so that all could fit. The light in the ceiling burned all the time. With no window, the men had no sense of day or night. There was no toilet, just a hole in the corner where fecal matter accumulated over months and left an intolerable stench. Food came twice a day in the form of a half a cup of rice and cabbage leaves, along with a ration of a cup of water. Almost daily, the guards would work their way down the hallway, enter each cell, and beat the prisoners.

If those beatings did not kill a man, it was assumed that some disease would. Tuberculosis, AIDS, dysentery, and countless other communicable diseases ravaged the prison. The cries of dying men would be followed by the silence of death. Lifeless naked bodies might sit for days before the guards would remove them. The extra space generated when a body was removed was but a temporary luxury, as new prisoners appeared regularly.

Initially, Reon reacted as anyone would if thrust into this nightmare. The hopelessness overwhelmed him. He found himself asking the God he thought he believed in the one question common to all who find themselves in despair: "Why me?" Reon remembers being consumed with that question one night when, suddenly, a Hagar the Horrible cartoon he had once seen popped into his head. In the cartoon, Hagar stands atop a mountain in a storm and shouts, "Why me?" In the next frame, a voice comes down from the heavens and replies, "Why not?"

On the verge of giving up, Reon found meaning in the most unlikely place. Though the hellish conditions in the prison cell had many sources, it was the hole in the ground that served as the toilet that truly bothered Reon. He could not stand the smell or sight of the feces-filled hole in the corner of the cell. Eventually, Reon realized he had the freedom to make a choice: either continue to be consumed by the thought and smell of the toilet, or clean it himself. He chose action and, one day, when the guards brought him his cup of water, he took it to the toilet hole and, using only his bare hands, cleaned out the fecal material. Reon recalled feeling fifty sets of eyes staring at his back as he worked. Soon Reon made cleaning the toilet hole part of his routine. Eventually, other prisoners followed his lead and began to take a turn cleaning the hole. The chore became a liberating act for the prisoners.

The constant hunger dominated the thoughts of the prisoners. The meager ration of a half cup of rice and cabbage leaves pushed the prisoners to the brink of starvation. After letting the hunger get the best of him for so long, Reon made a decision to remove thoughts of food from his mind. He slowly trained himself to forget about the desire for food. Eventually, he set his mind free from the bondage imposed by hunger. Though he had no control over when and what he ate, Reon no longer let the absence of food control him.

Hatred for his captors also nearly consumed him. How could it not? He had been thrust into an unimaginably inhumane existence, subjected to daily beatings, stripped of his clothing, and starved nearly to death. But Reon again realized the power of choice. He came to understand that by letting go of that hate and replacing it with an attitude of forgiveness, he would set himself free from his captors. Liberated from hate and thoughts of revenge, Reon found the inner peace he needed to not only survive, but to survive with a purpose.

The years of incarceration took their toll. As men around him became sick or died, Reon made the choice to offer comfort. But soon, Reon succumbed to illness. He was diagnosed with cancer by the prison doctors and was on several occasions taken in chains to a hospital for operations. After one such operation, he remembered waking up in shackles in the bed of truck, encircled by guards, heading down the dusty road back to the prison. Malnourished, surrounded by death and disease, left to bide his time naked in an overcrowded cell, his body riddled with cancer, Reon's situation seemed hopeless. Yet he persevered, relying on his belief in the power of choice to carry him forward.

Then, after twelve years in hell, the ordeal was over. The scene described at the start of this story unfolded because of the work of a support group that petitioned the leaders of South Africa to seek a pardon for Reon from Zimbabwe President Robert Mugabe. Eventually, Mugabe agreed to the pardon and at midafternoon on October 21, 2004, 43-year-old Reon Schutte emerged from hell.

The world he entered in 2004 was unknown to him. So much had changed, especially in his native South Africa. But Reon too had changed. He now regards his unimaginable ordeal as a gift, and he believes that he emerged from his captivity as the victor, not the victim. Forgiveness, faith, and the power of choice had set him free long before he walked out of Chikurubi in 2004. And despite battling cancer and despite the many physical and psychological scars from his imprisonment, Reon continues to preach that timeless message today.

Notes and Suggested Reading

Chapter One

❖ It is your care for others that is the true measure of your greatness.

Jesus of Nazareth

The quote is taken from Luke 9:48 according to the *Catholic Living Bible*. This is not a traditional rendering of the verse, but I chose this translation because of its directness and simplicity. Other translations convey this ideal of unconditional charity a bit more indirectly, relying on the context (the scene I depicted in the first dialogue of the book) to give meaning to the words of Jesus. For instance, in the *King James Version*, Jesus says this to his followers as he holds a child, a symbol of helplessness and vulnerability: "For he that is least among you all, the same shall be great." Other translations use similar wording. Of course, the actual words of Jesus of Nazareth are elusive. The "quest" for the real Jesus has been the subject of intense Biblical scholarship and the debate over the disparity between what the historical Jesus actually did and said and what early Christian writers claim he did and said has been particularly shrill in recent years. I am not qualified nor inclined to weigh in on that debate. For my purposes, any translation of this passage would have worked. I simply chose the most concise.

Borg, Marcus J. *Meeting Jesus Again for the First Time: the Historical Jesus & the Heart of Contemporary Faith*. San Francisco: Harper SanFrancisco, 1994.

Crossan, John Dominic. *Jesus: A Revolutionary Biography*. New York, NY: HarperOne, 2009.

Meier, John P. *A Marginal Jew: Rethinking the Historical Jesus*. Vol. I-III. New York: Doubleday, 1991.

Ratzinger, Joseph, and Benedict XVI. Pope. *Jesus of Nazareth*. New York: Doubleday, 2007.

There Is Room at the Inn

Ilibagiza, Immaculée, and Steve Erwin. *Left to Tell: Discovering God Amidst the Rwandan Holocaust*. Carlsbad, CA: Hay House, 2006.

Interview by Ed Gogan. *Www.npr.org*. National Public Radio, 10 Nov. 2009. Web. 22 Aug. 2011.

Rusesabagina, Paul, and Tom Zoellner. *An Ordinary Man: An Autobiography*. New York: Viking, 2006.

Could You Patent the Sun?

"Closing in on Polio." Time 29 Mar. 1954. Web.

"It Works." *Time* 25 Apr. 1955. Web.

Kluger, Jeffrey. *Splendid Solution: Jonas Salk and the Conquest of Polio*. New York: G.P. Putnam's Sons, 2004.

Smith, Jane S. *Patenting the Sun: Polio and the Salk Vaccine*. New York: W. Morrow, 1990.

Chapter Two

❖ A man's true wealth hereafter is the good he does in this world to his fellow man.

Muhammad

Muslims consider the Quran to be the word of God (or Allah) as revealed to Muhammad through the angel Gabriel. Sayings or teachings called hadith that are attributed to the Prophet also play a role in traditional Islam. Much like the words of Jesus of Nazareth, these sayings of Muhammad originally were passed down through an oral tradition before eventually being written down. I chose this particular saying because it redefines the term wealth, effectively turning it upside down. Wealth for most of us is measured by how much we have. Muhammad teaches that "true wealth" is measured by how much we care.

Armstrong, Karen. *Muhammad: a Prophet for Our Time*. New York: HarperOne, 2007.

Aslan, Reza. *No God but God: the Origins, Evolution, and Future of Islam*. New York: Random House Trade Paperbacks, 2006.

Father Damien and the Lepers of Kalaupapa

Cosgrove-Mather, Bootie. "Last Days of a Leper Colony." *CBSnews. com*. CBS News, Inc., 22 Mar. 2003. Web. 23 Aug. 2011.

Daws, Gavan. *Holy Man, Father Damien of Molokai*. Honolulu [Hawaii: University of Hawaii, 1984.

Stewart, Richard. *Leper Priest of Moloka'i: The Father Damien Story*. Honolulu: University of Hawai'i, 2000.

Tayman, John. *The Colony*. New York: Scribner, 2006.

American Moses

Bradford, Sarah. *Harriet Tubman: The Moses of Her People*. New York: Corinth Books, 1961.

Bradford, Sarah. *Scenes in the Life of Harriet Tubman*. Freeport: Books for Libraries Press, 1971.

Clinton, Catherine (2004). *Harriet Tubman: The Road to Freedom*. New York: Little, Brown and Company.

Larson, Kate Clifford. *Bound for the Promised Land: Harriet Tubman, Portrait of an American Hero*. New York: Random House, 2005.

Chapter Three

❖ Before you embark on a journey of revenge, dig two graves.

Confucius

What is known about Confucius is derived from sources that date centuries after his death. According to these sources, Confucius was an itinerant philosopher and teacher who developed a school of philosophy concerned with the role of individual thought and action (the concept of the ideal man) in the context of the greater society. This quote is simple and biting. The image of two graves is effective in emphasizing the dangers of retribution for both parties involved. The folly of revenge is addressed in several other teachings of Confucianism, including the image of the broken branch that I use in the scene I created.

Kaizuka, Shigeki. *Confucius: His Life and Thought*. Mineola, NY: Dover Publications, 2002.

Confucius, and Leonard A. Lyall. *The Sayings of Confucius.* Teddington Middlesex: Echo Library, 2008.

The Duel

Brookhiser, Richard. *Alexander Hamilton, American.* Free Press, 1999.

Chernow, Ron. *Alexander Hamilton.* The Penguin Press, 2004.

Ellis, Joseph J. *Founding Brothers: The Revolutionary Generation.* New York: Alfred A. Knopf, 2000.

Stewart, David O. *American Emperor: Aaron Burr's Challenge to Jefferson's America.* New York: Simon & Schuster, 2011.

Mob Justice

"Awful Crime at St. Elmo." *Chattanooga Times* 24 Jan. 1906.

"Feeling at High Pitch." *Chattanooga Times* 25 Jan. 1906.

"God Bless You All—I am Innocent." *Chattanooga Times* 20 Mar. 1906.

"Famous American Trials: The Trial of Sheriff Joseph Shipp, et.al." *UMKC.law.edu.* UMKC. Web. 3 Feb. 2010.

Chapter 4

❖ Let he who is without sin cast the first stone.

Jesus of Nazareth

Some readers might object to the inclusion of two quotes attributed to Jesus of Nazareth as an example of some sort of "Christian bias" in my thinking and writing. I must admit that at various points in my writing process, I considered omitted this saying, in order to avoid that appearance. In the end, though, I realized that I had to be true to the title of the book and include what I perceived as the most important things written or said, regardless of the source. Taken as a whole, the book does present a wide variety of sayings from diverse sources, all supported by stories from and about an assortment of people and places.

A couple of images stand out whenever I read this New Testament passage. First and foremost, I imagine a compassionate Jesus walking into a collection of self-righteous accusers who are surrounding a defenseless woman whom they perceive to be an unrepentant sinner. A clear dichotomy emerges in the scene: the powerful religious leaders robed in the finest linens set against the accused adulterer, a woman likely of meager means and questionable background, perceived as worthless and unclean. When Jesus does the unthinkable and shows preference for the accused, indignation and spite must have overwhelmed the accusers.

The second image is that of the accusers slowly walking away after Jesus challenges those with no sins to cast the first stone. The self-righteous accusers were dispersed not by force, but by their own hypocrisy. Incidentally, much has been written about the gospel description of Jesus writing in the dirt (the only mention in the gospels of Jesus writing anything). What was he writing? Did that cause the men to abandon the scene? I will leave that for others to debate.

Witch Hunt

Boyer, Paul S., and Stephen Nissenbaum. *Salem Possessed: The Social Origins of Witchcraft*. Cambridge, MA: Harvard UP, 1978.

Boyer, Paul S., and Stephen Nissenbaum. *The Salem Witchcraft Papers: Verbatim Transcripts of the Legal Documents of the Salem Witchcraft Outbreak of 1692*. New York: Da Capo, 1977.

Miller, Arthur. *The Crucible*. New York: Viking Penguin, 1954.

"Salem Witch Trials Documentary Archive and Transcription Project." University of Virginia. Web. 11 Feb. 2011.

Trask, Richard B. *The Devil Hath Been Raised: A Documentary History of the Salem Village Witchcraft Outbreak of March 1692:*

Together with a Collection of Newly Located and Gathered Witchcraft Documents. Danvers, MA: Yeoman, 1997.

Holy War

Giuliano, Michael James. *Thrice-born: The Rhetorical Comeback of Jimmy Swaggart*. Macon, GA: Mercer UP, 1999.

Harris, Art. "A Sleuth in the Louisiana Holy War: Snooping by Private Eye Led to Swaggart's Downfall." *Los Angeles Times* 22 May 1988.

Wright, Lawrence. *Saints and Sinners: Walker Railey, Jimmy Swaggart, Madalyn Murray O'Hair, Anton LaVey, Will Campbell, Matthey Fox*. New York: Vintage, 1993.

Chapter 5

❖ Sacred cows make the best hamburger.

Samuel Clemens

No list of quotes would be complete without something from the dry, sardonic wit of Samuel Clemens. I am a fan of all things Clemens. Even though it is unlikely he really said all the things attributed to him, no one can deny the genius of his writing. The following Clemens works are must reads: *Adventures of Huckleberry Finn, The*

Adventures of Tom Sawyer, Life on the Mississippi, The Celebrated Jumping Frog of Calaveras County and Other Sketches.

Powers, Ron. *Mark Twain: a Life*. New York: Free, 2006.

Zall, Paul M., and Mark Twain. *Mark Twain Laughing: Humorous Anecdotes by and about Samuel L. Clemens*. Knoxville: University of Tennessee, 1985.

You can have any color you want, as long as it is black

Bak, Richard. *Henry and Edsel: the Creation of the Ford Empire*. Hoboken, NJ: Wiley, 2003.

Brinkley, Douglas. "Prime Mover." *American Heritage* 2003 54(3): 44-53.

Watts, Steven. *The People's Tycoon: Henry Ford and the American Century*. New York: Vintage, 2006.

Outsmarting Big Blue

Howe, Carl. "Microsoft's Current Situation: Like IBM in the 80s" *Stock Market News & Financial Analysis—Seeking Alpha*. 26 July 2006. Web.

Manes, Stephen, and Paul Andrews. *Gates: How Microsoft's Mogul Reinvented an Industry and Made Himself the Richest Man in America*. New York: Simon and Schuster, 1994.

"The Long Shadow of Big Blue." *The Economist* (2002).

Wallace, James, and Jim Erickson. *Hard Drive: Bill Gates and the Making of the Microsoft Empire*. New York: HarperBusiness, 1993.

Chapter 6

❖ Gentleness, self-sacrifice and generosity are the exclusive possession of no one race or religion.

Mohandas Gandhi

The story of Gandhi and his shoes is a popular one. Though it is likely apocryphal, I use it here because it serves to set the context for the conversation I created to support the quote. Gandhi embodied the gentleness, self-sacrifice, and generosity he alludes to in the saying.

Gandhi, and Mahadev H. Desai. *An Autobiography: the Story of My Experiments with Truth*. Boston: Beacon, 1993.

Lelyveld, Joseph. *Great Soul: Mahatma Gandhi and His Struggle with India*. New York: Alfred A. Knopf, 2011.

Rushdie, Salman. "Mohandas Gandhi." *Time* 13 Apr. 1998. Web.

Corrie Ten Boom

Ten Boom, Corrie, Elizabeth Sherrill, and John L. Sherrill. *The Hiding Place*. Peabody, MA: Hendrickson, 2009.

Ten Boom, Corrie, and Jamie Buckingham. *Tramp for the Lord*. New York, NY: Jove, 1978.

Transcendent Peace

"Legacy." *Ibiblio—The Public's Library and Digital Archive*. 02 Sept. 2011. Web.

Quandt, William B. *Camp David: Peacemaking and Politics*. Washington, D.C.: Brookings Institution, 1986.

*The Origins of Sadat's Strategic Volte-face: (Marking 30 Years Since Sadat's Historic Visit to Israel, November 1977)*Israel Studies—Volume 13, Number 2, Summer 2008, pp. 28-53.

Chapter 7

❖ Treat the earth well: it was not given to you by your parents, it was loaned to you by your children.

Native American Proverb

The proverb succinctly expresses the unique respect that Native Americans have for the land, water, and air that sustains them. It is shameful and ironic that the only thing we did not take from Native American tribes was what would have benefitted us most: a love of and reverence for Mother Earth.

How to Make a Sea Disappear

Bissell, Tom (April 2002). "Eternal Winter: Lessons of the Aral Sea Disaster." *Harper's*: pp. 41-56.

Kozlava, Marina. "Coping with the Shrinking Aral Sea." *Businessweek—Business News, Stock Market & Financial Advice*. 12 Oct. 2006. Web.

Micklin, Philip and Nikolay V. Aladin (March 2008). "Reclaiming the Aral Sea." *Scientific American*.

The Death of Easter Island

Diamond, Jared. "Easter Island's End." *Discover Magaine*. August 1995. 16(8).

Ponting, Clive. *A Green History of the World: The Environment and the Collapse of Great Civilizations*. New York, NY: Penguin, 1993.

Rainbird, Paul. "A Message for Our Future? The Rapa Nui (Easter Island) Ecodisaster and Pacific Island Environments." *World Archaeology* Vol. 33, No. 3, Ancient Ecodisasters (Feb., 2002), pp. 436-451.

The Deadliest $1 Ever Spent

Beck, Eckard C. "The Love Canal Tragedy." *EPA Journal, January 1979.*

Engelhaupt, Erika. "Happy Birthday, Love Canal." *Environ. Sci. Technol.*, 2008, *42* (22), pp 8179-8186.

Environmental Protection Agency. *Ruckelshaus Denies Request to Buy Love Canal Homes. Www.epa.gov.* EPA, 2 Aug. 1984. Web.

Gibbs, Lois Marie., and Murray Levine. *Love Canal: My Story.* Albany: State University of New York, 1982.

Chapter 8

❖ In the End, we will remember not the words of our enemies, but the silence of our friends.

Martin Luther King

Martin Luther King is among the most oft-quoted figures of the twentieth century, and rightfully so. Like Gandhi, King is that rare leader who, through words and deeds, manages to transcend his particular cause. The quote I chose, though certainly applicable to the civil rights movement, is really a universal appeal to recognize and stand up against all forms of injustice. Silence is not an option. Like King, Pedro Arrupe, S.J., the famous Superior General of the Society of Jesus, expressed this call for action quite eloquently in the early 1970s when he said that "no longer are half measures and timid solutions admissible" in the fight for justice. No man better embodies the call for action in the face of injustice than King. And though it is said that actions speak louder than words, the power and grace of King's speeches and writings might be the exception.

King, Martin Luther, and Coretta Scott King. *The Words of Martin Luther King, Jr.* New York: Newmarket, 1987.

King, Martin Luther, and James Melvin. Washington. *I Have a Dream: Writings and Speeches That Changed the World.* [San Francisco]: HarperSanFrancisco, 1992.

A Simple Act

Berkow, Ira. "Standing Beside Jackie Robinson, Reese Helped Change Baseball." *New York Times* 31 Mar. 1997.

"Rachel Robinson Recalls How The Late Pee Wee Reese Helped Jackie Robinson Integrate Baseball." Jet. 13 Sep. 1999.

Robinson, Jackie, and Alfred Duckett. *I Never Had It Made: an Autobiography of Jackie Robinson.* Hopewell, NJ: Ecco, 1995.

The Genovese Syndrome

Davis, Linsey, Michael Milberger and Kate Santichen. "Good Samaritan Left for Dead on City Sidewalk." ABC News.com. 25 April 2010.

Gansberg, Martin. "Thirty Eight Who Saw Murder Didn't Call the Police." *New York Times* 27 March 1964.

Rosenthal, A. M. *Thirty-eight Witnesses: the Kitty Genovese Case.* Berkeley: University of California, 1999.

Sulzberger, A.G. and Mick Meenan. "Questions Surround a Delay in Help for a Dying Man." *New York Times* 25 April 2010.

<u>Chapter 9</u>

❖ You never really understand a person . . . until you climb into his skin and walk around in it.

Atticus Finch, <u>To Kill a Mockingbird</u>

In 2003, the American Film Institute released its list of the 100 top movie heroes of all time. Atop the list was Atticus Finch, a somewhat surprising choice given that our traditional perception of a movie hero is more along the lines of the tough-guy characters who filled in the rest of the list: Indiana Jones, Rocky, James Bond, etc. The subtle performance of Gregory Peck in the role of Atticus was flawless. In fact, the movie was a rarity: a classic work of literature translated into a classic movie. But, of course, the words attributed to Atticus Finch really belong to Harper Lee. Her first and only novel is, with apologies to Samuel Clemens, the Great American Novel.

Lee, Harper. *To Kill a Mockingbird.* Philadelphia: Lippincott, 1960.

The Same God Made Both of Us

Tibbles, Thomas Henry, and Kay Graber. *Standing Bear and the Ponca Chiefs.* Lincoln: University of Nebraska, 1995.

Starita, Joe. *I Am a Man: Chief Standing Bear's Journey for Justice.* New York: Griffin, 2010.

"Standing Bear's Victory." *Omaha Herald* 13 May 1879.

Executive Order 9066

Children of the Camps. Dir. Satsuki Ina. Center for Asian American Media, 1999.

Cogan, Frances B. *Captured: the Japanese Internment of American Civilians in the Philippines, 1941-1945.* Athens, GA: University of Georgia, 2000.

Executive Order 9066, February 19, 1942; General Records of the Unites States Government; Record Group 11; National Archives.

Personal Justice Denied. Wash., D.C.: Civil Liberties Public Education Fund, 1997.

Robinson, Greg. *By Order of the President: FDR and the Internment of Japanese Americans.* Cambridge, MA: Harvard UP, 2001.

Chapter 10

❖ Everything can be taken from a man but one thing: the last of the human freedoms—to choose one's attitude in any given set of circumstances, to choose one's own way.

Viktor Frankl

The circumstances that Frankl encountered as a prisoner in a concentration camp provide a context for the quote. It is impossible for me to truly comprehend the suffering and horror in such a setting. Few of us have had everything taken from us. I marvel at the strength of character of men and women who, having been thrust into hopeless circumstances, refuse to let those who oppress them, those who inflict physical and psychological wounds on them, those who harbor intense hatred for them, to ever truly have complete control over them.

A quick note on the story entitled "I Promise": This story has been told and written many times by many people. While it is difficult to verify the authenticity of all the facts, there is no denying the devastation of the Armenian earthquake, especially in Spitak. The poorly constructed buildings, including the school, were the primary reason why the death toll reached 25,000.

Survivors

Frankl, Viktor Emil. *Man's Search for Meaning*. Boston: Beacon, 2006.

Frankl, Viktor Emil. *The Will to Meaning: Foundations and Applications of Logotherapy*. New York, N.Y., U.S.A.: Penguin, 1988.

Wiesel, Elie. *Night*. New York: Bantam, 1982.

Wiesel, Elie, Richard D. Heffner, and Thomas J. Vinciguerra. *Conversations with Elie Wiesel*. New York: Schocken, 2003.

Wiesel, Elie. *All Rivers Run to the Sea: Memoirs*. New York: Knopf, 1995.

Downing, Frederick L. *Elie Wiesel: A Religious Biography*. Macon, GA: Mercer UP, 2008. Print.

Gulag

Ciszek, Walter J., and Daniel L. Flaherty. *With God in Russia*. San Francisco: Ignatius, 1997.

Ciszek, Walter J., and Daniel L. Flaherty. *He Leadeth Me*. San Francisco: Ignatius, 1995.

The Father Walter Ciszek Prayer League. 2008. Web. 28 Aug. 2011. <http://www.ciszek.org>.

Chikurubi

Schutte, Reon. "The Power of Choice." Embassy Suites, Omaha. 15 Dec. 2011. Speech.

"Zimbabwe releases apartheid-era spy to South Africa." *New Zimbabwe.com.* Web. 18 Sept. 2011.

Images

CPSIA information can be obtained at www.ICGtesting.com
Printed in the USA
LVOW051612190613

339337LV00006B/823/P